My

THE MESSI

I am in awe of the courage that Tracey Ricks has displayed in unveiling the intimate details of her life through the pages of her new book, *The Messed Up Missionary*. Tracey has persevered past the shame and stigma that often accompanies a history such as hers, to release a lifeline of freedom to many in the church who still need to be delivered.

The Messed Up Missionary will open the doorway for readers to recognize their own "messed up" situations that still need to be given over to GOD so that they can walk in the liberty that the completed work of Christ has already made available.

~ Dr. Kisia L. Coleman,
M.O.D.E.L. (Mentoring Our Daughters, Equipping Ladies) Ministries, Founder, Kingdom Church Int'l., Co-Founder, KishKnows, Inc., Book Publishing Coach & Self-Publishing Servicer, Chicago, IL.

THE MESSED UP MISSIONARY

Delivered from a Life of Sexual Perversion,
Abuse & Drug Addiction to Real Love,
Healing & Restoration

Tracey L. Ricks

Just for You Pastor Walker,
Blessings to you Woman of God! I
thank and I praise God for you
and for who you are in the Kingdom!
I am grateful for our Kingdom
connection! May the richest
abundant blessings of the Lord
continue to be your portion!
Much Love
always,
Tracey L. Ricks

KishKnows
PUBLISHING

The Messed Up Missionary – Delivered from a Life of Sexual Perversion, Abuse & Drug Addiction to Real Love, Healing & Restoration
by Tracey L. Ricks

Cover design, editing, book layout and publishing services by KishKnows, Inc., Richton Park, Illinois, 708-252-DOIT admin@kishknows.com, www.kishknows.com

ISBN 978-0-692-93972-7
LCCN 2017913627

Some Scripture references may be paraphrased versions or illustrative references of the author. Unless otherwise specified, all other references are from King James Version of the Bible.

Printed in the United States of America

ACKNOWLEDGMENTS

Before I do anything else, I first want to thank my Lord and Savior Jesus Christ for bringing me through so that I am even able to have a story to tell! Although you will read about some things that have happened in my life that I am not proud of, it is my story and I am grateful that the Lord never gave up on me.

"And they overcame him by the blood of the Lamb, and by the word of their testimony; and they loved not their lives unto death." (Revelation 12:11)

Thanks to all of my children, as I love them so very much. They, along with their father, are a very important part of my story.

I also want to thank all of my family and friends who have stood by me and have shown their support. I love you all!

I thank and I praise God for my spiritual mom, Mother Lisa Reynolds, who has encouraged me to share my story with the world. She has always been there for me, she prays for me and my family and supports me in my endeavors, and she always encourages and never judges me. She is an anointed woman of God who is powerful in prayer, strength, wisdom, and love, and I love her so much!

I have also received encouragement and support from my sister, Mrs. Judy A. Riley, who is both my prayer partner and confidant. She has stood by me and has been my sounding board and a true friend and sister by the blood of Jesus. 3/7 – 7/3!!!

I cannot forget my other sister, Ms. Rachel Peel, who listened to my every plight and offered wisdom nuggets that enabled me to press on in the wisdom of God. Our daily morning telephone chats are always a blessing and I love her from the bottom of my heart.

The Lord has used Dr. Juanita Bynum and Prophetess Sophia Ruffin countless times to send me confirmation about writing this book and being obedient so that my dream that had been buried a long time ago could be fulfilled, and I want to take this time to thank them both!

Lastly, I would like for everyone to know that you do not have to live in sin because the Lord Jesus Christ died and shed His blood that we can be free from sin. No matter what you have done, Jesus forgives you, Jesus can deliver you and Jesus will set you free!

That is why the word "Missionary" on the front cover of this book is highlighted in red because the blood of Jesus Christ covers and cleanses!

The Word of God says:

"For the thief cometh not, but for to steal,
and to kill, and to destroy:
I am come that they might have life,
and that they might have it more abundantly."
(John 10:10)

This day, choose Jesus and choose Life!

TABLE OF CONTENTS

INTRODUCTION

"Before I formed thee in the belly I knew thee; and before thou camest forth out of the womb I sanctified thee, and I ordained thee a prophet unto the nations."
(Jeremiah 1:5)

Even before I was born, the Lord knew the way that I would take. I was predestined before the foundation of the world, and He knew that I would experience abandonment, rejection, sexual abuse, physical abuse, bullying, drug addiction, lesbianism (both in and out of the church), promiscuity and self-gratification. Even though all of these things were a part of my life and He knew that they would be, He still chose me to be a Missionary!

James 1:13-14 says, **"Let no man say when he is tempted, I am tempted of God; for God cannot be tempted with evil, neither tempteth he any man: But every man is tempted, when he is drawn away of his own lust, and enticed."**

Most of the time we know the right way. Even if we are not saved, we still have a conscience and we know right from wrong. Isn't it amazing though, that the AWESOME GOD that we serve, loves us beyond our faults and our shortcomings and cares so much about us that He chastens us and continues to put us on the Potter's Wheel, that we might ultimately be the vessels that He desires us to be?!

This is my story... my testimony of what the Lord Jesus Christ has done in my life.

He took a wretch like me and He saved me, sanctified me, cleansed me, washed me, delivered me, restored me, called me to be a Missionary and loved me back to Himself so that He could get the glory out of my story! He took my mess and gave me a message and He made my *TEST* into a *TESTimony*! I was truly

THE MESSED UP MISSIONARY!!!

Chapter 1

THE CHILDHOOD YEARS

I remember growing up in the projects on the Northwest side of the Bronx when most people hadn't even heard of Marble Hill. Our neighborhood back then was approximately 65% Caucasian and 35% mixed between African Americans and Hispanics. It was the kind of neighborhood where you could get a ticket from Officer Hannon if you walked on the grass. I lived in an apartment with my grandmother (Nana), my grandfather (Pop-Pop), my mother, my older brother, and my sister. It was a little crowded, but we were family and we loved each other.

On Sundays, my mom used to send us to the Methodist church that we attended. We would always stop at the corner candy store first and spend some of the money that we were given to put in the Sunday School offering on candy. Sometimes, in the service, it was so embarrassing when Pop-Pop would start snoring while Pastor Tiek was delivering his message. Growing up, I never heard about salvation, baptism in Jesus' Name or receiving the gift of the Holy Ghost with the evidence of speaking in other tongues. I only knew about being christened, which is offering the baby back to the Lord. Once you were finished with "church duty" on Sunday, you did what you wanted and lived how you wanted during the rest of the week. Most of the time how you lived never really lined up with the Word of God.

"Tracey, come and put on your dress, your father is coming over to take us out!"

I can still see that white dress with the bib in the front and the ruffles around it. It had strawberries on it and two long ties on either side that my mom would tie in a bow behind my back.

It was the cutest thing! My dad loved that dress and almost every time he would come to visit us, my mom would make me put it on. My dad would come over and take us bowling, to the drive-in movie or to the Chinese restaurant to eat. I loved those times! Even though my brother and sister were not his biological children, he would take us all out and he loved them and treated them just like they were his own.

After a while, my dad just stopped coming around and I was heartbroken. I had no idea what happened — all I knew was that I didn't see him anymore. Nothing was ever explained to me and I would not find out until much later in my life what really happened.

Golden Nugget: Fathers, please continue to have a relationship with your children, even if things don't work out between you and their mother. A father/child relationship is so important and you will miss so much of your child's life by not being there! You should be the first example for your daughter of how she is supposed to be treated by a man, and the first example for your son of what a real man is and how he is supposed to act as a man, a husband, and a father. Mothers, please allow your child's father to have that relationship with his child, if it is not detrimental to the child.

In February of 1970, when my little brother was born, I moved to another building in the same development with my mom and my siblings because we needed more space since there was a new addition to the family. My brother was born prematurely, and his story, along with a picture of him and my mom, was featured in one of those parenting magazines. He and my mom were famous! My brother came home on my birthday and my mom allowed my birthday party guests to go into the room one at a time to see him.

One day, my uncle came over to visit and brought us a dog. She was adorable and we named her Lateef. Of course, back then you weren't allowed to have dogs in the projects, but everyone else broke the rules so why not us? Unfortunately, some of our nosy neighbors complained to housing that we had a dog and they gave my mother a hard time, so she made us give Lateef away. A young man named Jimmy, who lived in the next building, was now the proud owner of Lateef... but the dog wasn't having it! One night, someone called us on the intercom from downstairs and told us that our dog was in front of the building. What a smart dog she was... she had come home! We ran downstairs and got her and brought her back up to our apartment.

The very next day was a Tuesday and I remember it so clearly because it was my birthday. I came home from school to change into my Brownie uniform and I found it very strange that Lateef did not greet me at the door and jump on me like she always did. When I asked my mom where she was, she told me that the ASPCA came and picked her up.

I was heartbroken and devastated – not on my birthday! I cried like a baby and refused to even speak to my mother.

In school, the next day, I wrote my name as Tracey Ricks instead of Tracey Brown like I usually did. In my house, everyone's last name was Brown except mine and it always made me feel odd and left out. My mother had given me my father's last name. My teacher told me that I needed to make up my mind and decide whether I was going to be a Brown or a Ricks. For me, it usually depended on whether or not I was upset with my mother that day. It was at that time that I embraced being different and so from then on, Tracey L. Ricks it was, even though most people knew me as Tracey Brown and continued to address me by that name.

I remember never wanting to share my middle name, even with my friends, because I never liked it. We would all be together and everyone would have these really cute middle names. I always thought that my middle name was a boy's name and I would lie and say that my middle name was Lisa. It is actually Lee and I was told later by my dad that it was his mother's first name and that's how I got it. After I found out where it came from, I began to embrace it and be honest about what it was. Always embrace who you are because we are all special and unique in the sight of God!

Growing up, I was always smart and was placed in the top classes where most of my friends were white. This caused me to get picked on a lot by some of my Black neighborhood friends. "In school, you always want to hang with them, but at home, you always want to hang with us. You need to make up your mind!" They were right. In school, I liked to hang with my white friends because they didn't get into trouble. We played in the yard and had a good time. Unfortunately, they mostly lived in Riverdale (an affluent part of the Bronx) and since they weren't around my neighborhood on the weekends, I hung with my "homies."

As a young girl, I had a very bad case of eczema. I used to break out with bumps on my arms and legs in the summertime. One year, I had a bad rash around my mouth and my so-called friends used to make fun of me and call me Rashy, Ashy Tracey. That used to eat me up. Sometimes, people can be so cruel! It didn't do a thing for my self-esteem.

There was a girl at school who really didn't like me, and there were many times when I was threatened in the schoolyard during recess. "I better not see you after school or I'm gonna whip your butt!" Most of the time it was for no reason at all, just because she was a bully and she knew that I was scared. When that happened, I would go back to the classroom and tell my teacher that I was sick and needed to go home. I did not want to get beat up after school in front of all my friends, and besides, I wasn't a fighter and I wasn't raised to fight people. I couldn't leave school sick all the time to avoid fights, and my mother was sick and tired of seeing me coming home crying after getting beat up. She told me, "If you come home crying one more time and don't fight her back then I'm going to whip your tail!"

One Sunday, I went on a bus trip to Pennsylvania Dutch Country with my mom and some other people. My mother purchased some cute little hanging earrings for me that were shaped like "clogs" or "Dutch shoes."

On Monday when I went to school, you couldn't tell me that I wasn't cute! I had on my pretty yellow dress with the white lace that showed my little shape, some white patent leather platform shoes, my light blue Easter coat with the plastic large white zipper down the front and my brand-new earrings. I was walking home from school by myself and I could hear the crowd behind me saying, "Get her, go ahead, push her!" I was as scared as I-don't-know-what but I was certainly not looking forward to a beating from my mother! I threw my book bag on the ground, kicked off my shoes and pulled off my coat. I turned around and looked her straight in the eye and said, "Okay 'B' ... you want to fight?" We went at it and I beat her tail! Scratched her face and everything. I went upstairs the victor and told my mother that I finally stood up to the bully and whipped her tail! The next day she told one of my classmates that her cat scratched her and she didn't even have one.

<u>Golden Nugget:</u> I do not condone fighting and there is no excuse for bullying. You just never know what a person is going through.

"If it be possible, as much as lieth in you, live peaceably with all men."
(Romans 12:18)

In elementary school, I was a cheerleader for the boys' basketball team. *"Ola, Ola A, Ola, Ola A, rolling, rolling, rolling chica boom, now, rolling, rolling, rolling, chica boom now, I don't know what is y'all, but it sure is funky. Ola Ola A, Ola Ola A, boom, boom, sure is funky now, boom, boom, score them points now, boom, boom, sure is funky now, boom, boom, make the other team look like clowns!"*

We had red flair skirts (that my mom made) and we wore them with yellow turtlenecks as our uniforms. My mom was an excellent seamstress — in fact, my mom used to make most of our clothes to save money, especially at Easter time. One year she even made matching three-piece suits for myself and one of my friends. We were styling and you couldn't tell us nothing!

I was beginning to get a little older now, and that shape of mine was beginning to fill out and make me noticeable. Maybe a little too noticeable for my own good, because that's when a member of my family inappropriately touched me. I was embarrassed and ashamed, but I told my mother what happened. Nothing ever came of it so I didn't know if maybe she didn't believe me... and so it began.

Chapter 2

THE TEENAGE YEARS

"Ring O Leevia one, two, three. Ring O Leevia, one, two, three, one, two, three! Dang, caught again!"

"Ring O Leevia" was one of the many games that we used to play growing up in the Hill. I was never really fast at running, so I would always get caught early in the game. We also used to play "Round-Up," where everyone would go and hide (usually in Buildings One, Two and Three) but you couldn't go up the stairs. One person would be "it" and they would have to find the others and round them up until everyone was found!

"RCK" ("Run, Catch and Kiss") was also a very popular game that everyone loved to play. I remember one time in particular. I got caught by this guy that we hung out with but I refused to kiss him because unfortunately, he was not so "on point" when it came to personal hygiene. I cried and almost wound up getting into a physical fight with him because I refused to kiss him and was therefore not being fair in playing the game.

Running relay races around the middle grass was always the main event. It would mostly happen at night and we had such a good time hanging out and having good clean fun. When the girls got together "Double Dutch" it was, and we could jump for hours on end. We played in teams or individually. If you could do the "crisscross" while you were in the ropes, you were something else! What a time we used to have.

Those were the days when you went upstairs at 6:00 to eat dinner, and if you came back outside, either your mother would call out the window when it was time to come upstairs (I lived on the thirteenth floor, but my mom had a really loud voice!) or you were told to come up when the street lights came on.

During the week, the community center was open after school. That was where we went and did our homework and then participated in the various programs that were offered. I remember one time my mom was teaching a sewing class. A lot of my friends enrolled and so did I, but for some reason, I never finished the class and I never learned how to sew. I wish that I did though. I could hem a pair of pants, sew on a button or sew up a hole, but that was about it.

I think that at that time my interest was beginning to turn more toward the opposite sex and that's where I began to focus. I had my eyes on this cutie who was the best friend of my friend's boyfriend. I was fourteen at the time and beginning to smell myself, thinking that I was grown. There were a lot of rumors going around about me, like I was easy, but they were all lies. I had never gone all the way with anyone! A little tongue kissing and feels here and there, but never all the way.

One day we all played hooky from school — my girlfriend, her boyfriend, my cutie and me. We went to my house since nobody was home and I had two bedrooms in my apartment. She and her boyfriend were in one bedroom, and the cutie and I were in the other. I was scared as I don't know what, but I couldn't let on to it.

I needed to at least act like I knew what I was doing. After it was all over and he saw the blood on the sheets, he knew everyone else had been lying. He really was my first one! I found out later that sex was all he wanted and he really didn't like me. He just wanted to see if what he had heard about me was true. I was devastated.

When it seemed to take longer than normal for my period to come, right away I thought that I might be pregnant. When I told him my concerns, he was so angry. "Well, you know if you are, you're not keeping it, right?" I told him I didn't know. For some strange reason, I thought that this might be a good way to keep him. After my period came, I decided that there was no need to string him along. If he didn't want to be with me for me, then a baby certainly wasn't going to make him stay. He was so relieved when I told him, and I was so hurt. Here I was thinking that this guy really liked me, but instead, I was just being used. This is one of the reasons that the Lord wants us to wait until marriage before we become intimate with someone. Years later, when we were grown, I had the opportunity to see this young man again. To my surprise, he apologized to me for taking my virginity and for the part he had played in what happened. I forgave him.

"Flee fornication. Every sin that a man doeth is without the body; but he that committeth fornication sinneth against his own body." (1 Corinthians 6:18)

I was sitting outside on the logs one day with my closest friend and she asked me, "Do you ever think of what happens to us after we die?" I said, "Nope, never gave it much thought." I'm not sure what made her ask me that, but years down the road, she was the first to get saved and filled with the Holy Ghost and was instrumental in inviting me to church which ultimately led to my salvation. But so much more happened before that.

When I was in junior high, I was with the same crew from elementary school – my friends from the "hood." Most of my white classmates went to junior high up in Riverdale. They didn't dare go to the same school that I went to because it was too bad over there. Growing up I seemed to always get into a lot of "he said/she said" stuff. You know, when somebody tells you something but you don't think that they were telling you because it is a secret, so then, you mention it to somebody else in a casual conversation. The next thing you know, it gets back to the person that told you and now it's time to fight again. Well, that same bully that used to fight me in elementary school must have been so angry that I got the last licks, so she started up with me again. Sometimes I ran home at lunchtime, sometimes I didn't. Sometimes she won and sometimes I did. No matter who won the fight, by the next day or so we were always friends again, because that's what friends do, right?

Golden Nugget: Please stay away from "he said/she said" drama. If anyone tells you something, even if you don't think that it was in confidence, keep it in confidence anyway! Don't share it!

More times than not it always gets twisted and never gets back the same way. Take it from me... DON'T DO IT!!!

"A talebearer revealeth secrets: but he that is of a faithful spirit concealeth the matter." (Proverbs 11:13)

"And that ye study to be quiet, and to do your own business, and to work with your own hands, as we commanded you." (1 Thessalonians 4:11)

Some of you may not have even known that these Scriptures were in the Bible!

"Mom, I don't feel well today – my stomach hurts so bad. Can I stay home?"

"Yeah, alright Tracey, but tomorrow you are getting out of here and going to school!"

That afternoon when my mother came home from work, she told me that she heard that all my friends just got caught playing hooky from school. She said, "I'm so glad that I knew that you were home sick today. All of your friends got caught playing hooky from school."

"Really? Well, I'm glad that you knew I was home sick!"

The very next day, we decided to play hooky and go to a friend's house. We were dancing and having a good time until some of the guys went outside and found someone to buy some vodka for them. They came back from the store and started drinking it like it was water, then they all got drunk, and somehow or another wound up in the staircase throwing up and making a lot of noise.

One of the neighbors called the cops, and after we were all back in the apartment, there came a knock at the door. "Police, open up!" Everyone ran and began to hide under the beds, in the closets, in the bathtub and anywhere that we could, because we were so scared. At first, my friend didn't want to open the door, but the policeman yelled, "If you don't open this door I'm going to bust it down!" My friend wound up opening the door and the officer came inside. I don't know how he knew that we were all in there, but he made everyone come out. He called my friend's mother at work and told her that she had a bunch of kids in her apartment playing hooky and drinking alcohol. When she came home, she made her son tell her the names of everyone that was there.

Fortunately, she did not have my telephone number, but she called the parents of everyone else who had been in her house playing hooky. When my phone rang, it was my friend's father. I was so glad that I had answered the phone.

"Hello?"

"Hello, Tracey? Where is your mother?"

I told him, "She's not here right now."

Then my mother yelled, "Tracey, who is that on the phone?"

He said, "Tracey put your mother on this phone right now!"

I said, "Okay... Ma, it's for you."

When my mother got off the phone, she came into my room with the belt in her hand. She immediately started swinging and I got a lash for every single syllable that came out of her mouth. I don't think that I played hooky again after that, or if I did, I never got caught again!

By this point, I had experienced abandonment, sexual abuse, being bullied, being used and having a big mouth! And the saga continues...

One night, I was at a basketball game and I caught the eye of this really cute guy. His face was chiseled and I could tell that he was older. He was the coach of the other team, and after the game, he came over to me and we started talking. He had a toothpick in his mouth and you know I was getting my flirt on hard! We exchanged numbers and said that we would keep in touch. I was sixteen at the time and he was nineteen – I had me an older man y'all! He lived downtown in Harlem, somewhere that I never really hung out.

The first couple of months to almost a year seemed to go pretty well between us. My mother seemed to like him and we really had a good time together – until he hit me. Sometimes we would get into arguments because he was extremely jealous. He didn't want any other guys to look at me or talk to me or anything. If we went to a party together, he was the only one that I was allowed to dance with. The first couple of times that he hit me, I kind of shrugged it off because I really liked him.

Of course, it was natural for couples to fight, argue and make up, right? This was my first real relationship so I didn't know what to expect. The making up was always the best part since I still hadn't learned my lesson, and I became sexually active with him.

When the seasons were changing from summer to fall and it was almost time to go back to school, my mother had me trying on my clothes from last year to see if they still fit. She noticed a little bulge in my stomach and said, "Why is your stomach sticking out like that girl, you pregnant?" I was so scared because I thought that I might be, so I told her the truth and said, "I'm not sure." The very next day I was at Planned Parenthood to take a pregnancy test. Sure enough, it came back positive. I remember sitting in the waiting area and she handed me a book entitled, *Getting an Abortion in New York City.* There was no discussion and she never asked me what I wanted to do – the decision had been made for me. They made an appointment for me to come back to have the procedure done. I didn't know that they were not going to put me to sleep and so I couldn't do it. I cried like a baby. They scheduled me for another day so that they could put me under and when I woke up I just cried and felt so empty inside.

I knew my boyfriend was angry that I had it done because he didn't have any say in the matter, but we continued to see each other. His mother loved me and told him that he better act right toward me and keep me because I was such a nice girl! I don't remember what sparked our last argument, but I do remember that he had come to the neighborhood to see me, and his nephew was with him.

His nephew was only about a year younger than he was. I met them at the train station and we walked through the park. We sat down on the bench and began to talk. After a while, he got up and said that he was going to the store and would be right back. He asked me to hold his jacket for him, which I did.

When he came back from the store, he stopped at the bench right before the one where I was sitting and started talking to this other girl. What in the world!? Oh no, you are not going to dis me like that! I went over to where he was, threw him his jacket and told him that it was over. Shoot, I didn't even have no father to put his hands on me, so I was totally done! His nephew walked me upstairs and I willingly allowed him to take advantage of this situation and kiss me. Oh my goodness, what was I doing? Huh, that boy was fine! The nephew and I dated for a little while, but we never went all the way. Eventually, I came to my senses and cut it off. I didn't want to start a family feud!

After those relationships ended, I found myself liking this guy that lived in my grandmother's building. His face was really square in shape, and he wore these wire-rimmed glasses. He wasn't necessarily my type, but he was paying attention to me and I liked it. He was the cousin of one of the girls that I went to school with. We were never intimate with each other, but he was a good kisser!

One day, he told me to go upstairs to his house and wait for him because he had something for me. He assured me that he would be there soon. I went upstairs to his apartment, and his brother was there.

From what I can remember, his brother was not all that stable. When I rang the doorbell, he opened the door and told me to come in. I explained to him that his brother told me to come up and wait for him and that he would be there shortly. He said okay, but he had this really strange look on his face when he closed the door. He locked it and then looked at me and said, "I've been waiting to get you someplace by yourself." I was so scared and I knew that I had to get out of there. I went to grab the doorknob, and it came off in my hand! It was like a scene from a horror movie! I told him that he better open that door before I start screaming. He laughed in a most frightful way and let me out of the house, and I ran down the stairs. I wasn't at all interested in waiting for the elevator! When I told his brother what had happened, he kind of just shrugged it off and said, "Well, you know my brother's crazy." That was enough of that for me and the relationship came to an abrupt end!

Now that I was in high school and he was a thing of the past, it was time for me to really get focused on my school work. Sometimes all that I could think about was whether the baby that I had aborted was a boy or a girl.

One day, in September of 1978, as I was going up the escalator at school, I began to walk up because I was in a hurry trying to get to class. There was this guy behind me and at first, I really didn't pay attention to how he looked — I just knew that I looked cute with my tight dark blue Jordache jeans. They had a blue and yellow design on the back pockets and I had on a yellow turtleneck to match.

As I was walking up the escalator trying to switch my rear, I tripped and began to fall up the steps! (How do you fall up the steps, right?) Well, the guy behind me grabbed me and said, "Don't fall now, but if you do, I'll definitely catch you!" He was with one of his friends and we all just laughed about it.

When I got to class and took my seat, a few seconds later, guess who comes walking in the room? The guy that just caught me falling up the steps! This time I was able to get a really good look at him and he was finnneeee!!!! Dark chocolate with a mustache, impeccably dressed and he even had dress shoes on! My God, this was class! Most guys in high school wore sneakers, but this one right here!

He saw me sitting in the class but the seat next to me was taken. We kept eyeing each other in the classroom, even though he had to look behind him in order to see me. Apparently, he was still in school doing an extra six months so that he could graduate. The teacher already knew his name and kept telling him to pay attention, because he was so busy looking at me. He waited for me after class and we exchanged numbers. I had no idea what I was in for. Just as we had said, we kept in touch and were calling each other on the phone almost every night. We would see each other in class and I would always save that seat next to me if I got to class first. We would talk to each other so much that the teacher would yell at us for being disruptive. He started bringing a steno notebook with him to class and we would write each other notes in the book and pass it back and forth so we wouldn't talk and get into trouble. Things were really starting to get serious!

He would come to my house and I would go to his. He had a large family, with eight children and his mother and father. I thought it was such a blessing to have a mother and father in the same house! One of his sisters even had the same name as me. There were two sets of twins in his family — one set was identical and one set was fraternal. The identical set of twins were girls and the fraternal set was a boy and a girl.

We always had so much fun at his house, because his mom would play music and we would dance and have a good time. In that house, they loved to cook and I loved to eat! Things were going great.

Of course, after a while, the inevitable came up. All of that kissing and feeling, it was bound to be addressed. I explained to him that I had been in a few bad relationships where I felt that I had given myself too quickly. This time I wanted to wait and make sure that he wanted to be with me for who I was and not for what I could give him. He said that he understood, and so we waited. I wanted to give us at least six months into the relationship before I became intimate with him. I thought that was enough time, but then again, what did I know? I myself had a hard time waiting and so in February of 1979, we began to get really serious and it was time to give in.

I was experiencing a lot of itching in my lower region and did not know what was going on. In the bathroom one day, I looked down and saw something crawling on me. My God, what in the world was this? After a visit to the doctor, I was diagnosed with my very first STD. I had crabs. I could not believe it. I certainly could not be intimate with him now. I had to tell him. I was so embarrassed, but even through that, he stuck by me and helped me get through it. I pretty much knew where it came from and I had to tell him too. I was livid! One thing I knew for sure though, he really cared about me and was concerned about me, so that was a good sign! He really did want me for me and not for what I was able to give him.

Our first attempt at intimacy was unsuccessful. It was snowing hard outside, but we had plans! He had picked up the bottle and the weed and we were on our way to an empty apartment that we had access to. We took a cab way across town and were excited about our very first time. Although it didn't happen, we still were able to talk, laugh and share while holding each other and we still enjoyed intimacy without physical interaction. He was so disappointed and I stood by his side and encouraged him through it all. But when it did happen, boy oh boy! Sometimes when he would come over, we would go downstairs to one of my neighbor's house that lived on the eighth floor. She was so cool! We would go down to her house and listen to music and smoke weed. Sometimes when she would go away, she would give me the keys and let me house sit, and what a time we would have.

I remember one time when I was coming home on the train, I ran into this guy from the neighborhood. We didn't really hang out, but I knew who he was. I was having a really bad day and he offered me some angel dust. I had never tried it before, but I was in such a bad mood that I thought, "Oh well! Whatever!" We went between the cars and smoked it.

When I got off that train and was walking home, I was so high! I knew that I was walking but it felt like the ground was just moving under my feet. I couldn't go home like this, so I went to my older friend's house that lived on the eighth floor. I called my mother on the intercom to let her know that I was going to stop at my friend's house. When I got upstairs, I told my older friend what happened and she said, "Girl, you need some milk to bring that high down!" I really didn't like milk that much but if it was the only thing that could help me, I had to do it. I must have had about three glasses before I began to feel better and the high began to subside. When I went upstairs to my house my mother never knew what had happened, and I never smoked dust again!

"Alright everybody, come out of this bathroom and I want to see everyone's pass!" It was the female dean, busting the girls' bathroom. It was my eighteenth birthday and I had on this cute black pleated dress that my mother had made for me with a thin silver belt around the waist. My hair was done and I was looking cute! I had cut her class fourth period, and it was now the sixth period when I had lunch and I was in that bathroom smoking cigarettes and weed and drinking vodka. At lunchtime, music would be played in the lunchroom and we never wanted to go back to class after lunch.

When I came out of the bathroom as high as a kite, the dean said, "Ms. Ricks you weren't in my class today, what happened?" I looked at her and said, "I'm sorry! Today is my birthday!" With that, she replied, "I don't care if it is your birthday, don't you ever cut my class again or I will call your mother!" I was so grateful that even though she blew me up, she still let me slide! She and I were cool. She was a Black teacher and I had her class for Data Processing. Her class was on the fourth floor and it was after my World History class on the seventh floor. By the time I got to her class, I could never get a working

DP machine so she would allow me to sit in the front with her and mark papers from her other classes. I passed her class with a 75, and I was happy just to pass!

I think it was that same year when I failed three major subjects – Math, Spanish and English. For Math, I was taking Geometry and I just couldn't get it. I had my homeroom teacher for that class. He said, "Tracey, you're such a nice girl, but you're just not getting it. I'm sorry but I have to give you a failing grade." That was the first time that a teacher ever apologized for failing me. I appreciated it though and even respected him for doing that. My Spanish teacher was crazy. The first day of class she was talking to us in Spanish like we were supposed to understand what she was saying! That class was a disaster from day one! I was so angry with her, that I remember seeing her one day at the train station after school. She thought that I was going to push her onto the tracks, so she stood way in the middle of the platform. In English class, I just couldn't seem to make sense of Shakespeare. I hated it and couldn't understand why we even had to learn that stuff. I decided that I just wouldn't participate and so, of course, I failed that class.

When my mother saw my report card, she was so disappointed in me, and I was so disappointed in myself. I was in this hot and heavy relationship and my focus had shifted. I then began to think of the fact that I had met this wonderful guy while he was doing an extra six months and I did not want that to be my fate. I wanted to graduate on time! I refocused and went to summer school to make up those classes. I took Business Math, which was fairly easy to make up for the Math class that I had failed. I had a Spanish class with a Black teacher who was far better than the female Spanish teacher that I had at school, and the English class was a writing class. I loved to write so I passed that with flying colors. Now that I was back on track, I was able to graduate on time.

At the end of the year, before graduation, we were preparing for our prom. I was so excited! My mom had made my dress and it was beautiful! It was a rusty orange color and it had silver stitching. It had a large strap over the left shoulder and the other shoulder was bare. The stitching on the shoulder strap was the same stitching on the wide belt that was around my waist and it was so long and flowed to the ground. My hair was braided with ornaments on the ends of them, and I had bangs. I thought I looked like Cleopatra!

My mother had rented a car to take us to the prom, which was being held at the Waldorf Astoria. I was in the house waiting for my date to come so that we could leave. It was getting late and I was beginning to get upset because I didn't want to miss the food that we had paid so much for. When my date arrived at my house, he was as drunk as a skunk. I mean really drunk!!!

I was so disappointed and upset that I almost didn't even want to go at that point, but he assured me that he would be okay, so we went. My mother and sister were in the car and we got lost. By this time, I was in tears and my mascara was starting to run. We finally made it, and I thanked God that we had not missed the food!

At the prom, one of my classmates had her cousin as her date. I used to date him, (the guy with the square face and wire-rimmed glasses) but it was never really anything serious and we had never gone all the way. He was just a crush. Well, my date knew that I used to see this guy, so when it was time to take our pictures, he wanted to show off and be a big shot, and also try to make up to me for what he had just put me through, so he purchased the whole set of our prom pictures. It did make me feel better. We danced the night away and had a great time at the after-party! I had brought a change of clothes with me for the after-party — a pair of hot pink Gloria Vanderbilt jeans with white piping down the sides and a short-sleeved hot pink and white Gloria Vanderbilt shirt to match. I was looking cute and you couldn't tell me nothing! After the after-party, we all went to IHOP for breakfast, and I think I got home about 9am the next morning.

Because my mother loved my boyfriend so much, sometimes she would let him spend the night and sleep on the couch. I'm pretty sure that she would do this because she was a token booth clerk and had to be at work very early in the morning. She had to leave the house around 5am, and she would wake him up and he would walk with her to the train station and she would let him get on the train for free. She didn't know that he would get off at one of the stations where he could just cross over the bridge and get the train going back uptown and come back to the house! Boy, the things we used to do!

One April, we made plans to go on a weekend trip with my sister and her boyfriend. Two of my sister's friends were also going with us. I remember my boyfriend's mother asking me, "Does your mother know that the two of you will be staying in the room together?"

I said, "Yes, ma'am, I guess she does since my sister and her boyfriend and two of her female friends are going and will stay in the room together."

"Well, alright then as long as she knows. Y'all are over eighteen and y'all are grown but mind yourselves, hear?!"

We had such a good time on that trip! We went horseback riding, and I remember us having drinks with our pancake breakfast. Who does that? We did! One morning though, I was as sick as a dog and really couldn't enjoy myself. He stayed in the room with me the whole time and took care of me. That was love!

After graduating from high school, I started working full-time at a law firm on Third Avenue in Manhattan. I got the job when I was in high school as a part of the co-op program. I was a file clerk and I did my job well — so well, in fact, that I was able to be hired full-time. I did not have any health benefits but it was okay because my mother had me on her plan.

When I was working at this job and still in school, I walked the same route every day. I believe that someone must have been watching me because one day as I was walking, this guy ran up to me and snatched my gold medallion and chain from around my neck. I was devastated as it was real gold! The fact remained though, that it was only a material thing and I was grateful that I had not been hurt in the process!

I had decided to go to college, and although I preferred to go away, I was still in a relationship with my high school sweetheart and did not want to leave him, so I chose to go to college in the city and was accepted to Baruch College. At first, I was going to take a break before going to college, but I decided against it because I did not want to get comfortable in a job, knowing that I would not go to school if I started making money.

While I was in school, during my freshman year, I found out that my mother was terminally ill with colon cancer. I lost focus again because there was so much on my mind. I took days off to stay home with my mom when she was sick and then on top of that I found out that I was pregnant! I refused to have another abortion since this time I felt like I had a say in the matter.

My mother knew that she wouldn't be around too much longer, so she was okay with me having the baby. The baby's father thought that he was too young to be a dad but I was adamant about not having another abortion. The mental stress was just too much! I wound up dropping out of school and received an "Incomplete" for all of my classes. I decided that I would go back later when I had things more together. I ended up having to leave my job because they said that they could not guarantee that it would be there for me after I had the baby, so I applied for public assistance.

At just nineteen years old, I had a beautiful baby boy! I can remember when my mother and my grandmother came to the hospital after he was born. My mother had lost so much weight and her skin had turned very dark because of the chemotherapy. She had lost her hair and did not resemble the lady that I knew to be my mother. I was glad to see them, but my heart was so heavy seeing her in that condition. I can still remember one day when I came home from school and she was sitting in the bathroom crying because she was in so much pain. I felt so helpless because there wasn't anything that I could do for her.

After I was released from the hospital and brought the baby home, my mother used to have me bring him to her and lay him next to her just so that she could enjoy his company and look at him. "Tracey, bring me the baby." She would call out to me from her room.

"But Mommy, he's sleeping now."

"I don't care, bring him anyway!" So, I would bring him to her room and lay him down next to her.

My Spanish next-door neighbors always went to church and the lady always wore long dresses and no makeup or jewelry. They were such very nice people. I had told her that my mother was very sick and asked her to pray for her. She did much more than that.

One night, the doorbell rang and it was my neighbor. She had brought her pastor and some of her church members to my house to pray for my mother. The pastor anointed my mother with oil and we all held hands. The pastor asked my mother if she would accept Jesus into her heart and she nodded her head yes. By this time, she couldn't even speak. Her eyes were protruding out of their sockets and I felt so bad for her and what she was going through. The pastor and the church members began to pray and they started speaking in another language that didn't sound like Spanish. I would find out later that they were speaking in tongues. When he ended the prayer with "Hallelujah," that was the only thing that sounded a little familiar to me as Hallelujah is the same in any language! I felt so much better after they had come and offered up prayers for my mom.

The night that my mother passed away, my family and I were all in the house and one of my neighbors came over to offer her condolences. She was a wonderful woman and we spent a lot of quality time at each other's houses. Sometimes I would babysit for her boys. She was newly saved and would sometimes talk to me about the Lord. We were going to the store to get some ice since people were coming to the house, and while we were walking she said to me, "You know that your mother didn't make it to Heaven, right?"

I said, "Yes, she did, why would you say that?"

She replied, "Because she smoked cigarettes up until she couldn't anymore and didn't have a chance to repent."

My heart dropped and I did not want to believe what she was saying. All I could see was my mother nodding her head yes when the pastor asked her if she would accept the Lord Jesus Christ as her Savior. My mother went to Heaven and you couldn't tell me anything different!

Chapter 3

THE PARENTING YEARS

I was a mother at nineteen years old and my mother passed away when my son was just nineteen days old. What was I to do? I didn't really know how to cook, clean house, pay bills or be a mother. My dinner was done at 6:00 every day when my mother was alive. I could cook some things, like hamburgers or franks, maybe even a steak and French fries or some fried fish.

My mother used to have fried fish and Lyonnaise potatoes almost every Friday and her friend Ms. Yvonne used to come over. I can remember one Friday night after we all had finished eating and my mother and Ms. Yvonne both lit up their after-dinner cigarettes. I asked my mother if I could light mine up too. I was about sixteen at the time. She said, "Girl, you better get out of my face asking me can you smoke." I decided to take advantage of the situation since she had company and lit my cigarette. I started blowing smoke rings and my mom and Ms. Yvonne started laughing, and Ms. Yvonne said, "Look Jan, she's even blowing smoke rings!" From that day on, I had permission to smoke cigarettes in the house.

Like I said, I didn't know how to be a homemaker and mother. My grandmother stayed with me for at least a month so that she could help me take care of my newly inherited apartment and baby. Since I was not twenty-one years old yet, my sister co-signed for me to stay in the apartment. She had moved out in 1975 when my grandfather passed away from walking pneumonia so that Nana wouldn't be by herself.

She also took my little brother over there with her after my mother died because I could barely take care of myself and my newborn baby, so how would I be able to take care of my little brother? I think my older brother was away at college or some type of program away from home at the time. A little while after Nana left, my baby's daddy moved in.

I benefited greatly from him being there because he knew how to cook, he knew how to clean and he would help out with the laundry, food shopping and help me take care of our son. He had a good paying job at a car dealership and we were doing well. What more could I ask for? We loved each other, but most of our arguments would be because I didn't take time to keep our house clean while he was out working. I would try to cook a meal for us, but it was hard trying to take care of the baby, keep the apartment clean, cook and keep up with my soap operas!

I was trying as hard as I could to be a good mother to my son, and keep his daddy happy. I don't know if I should place some of the blame for not wanting to cook and keep the house clean on the way that I was raised, but it sure caused a lot of friction in our home. He liked a clean apartment and I was just content with being in an apartment. I still had a lot of things on my mind — I had lost my mom at a young age and I didn't feel equipped to carry all of the responsibility that had just been dumped in my lap.

After my mom passed away, I tried to find my dad. I felt like he needed to know that my mother was gone. I didn't know where to start to look for him and the only information that I had was what was on my birth certificate. I only knew that his occupation was a beef boner and his age at the time that I was born. I began to reach out, writing a letter to Oprah Winfrey and questioning my family members about him to try and get more information. I never received a reply from Oprah and the little information that my family had, could not help me find him.

After a while, I became discouraged about the whole situation and so I gave up. I wondered where he was, why he had been missing all of this time, and why he didn't even care enough to come and see me. He knew my grandmother's telephone number because it had never changed. All of these things were going through my mind and caused me to start to be bitter, so I tried to put everything out of my mind, at least for a while.

The arguments became a little more intense between my boyfriend and me, and I noticed that he was beginning to drink a little more and stay out a little later after work. I knew it couldn't be because of the way I looked, because exactly one week after I had given birth, I was back in my Jordache jeans! Even when I was pregnant, guys would see me from the back and start trying to rap to me. It was only when I turned around and they saw my big stomach that they would then apologize to me for being disrespectful. I really didn't have too much to complain about. He was working a good job, bringing home the money, doing the grocery shopping, cleaning the house, doing the laundry, cooking the food and helping me take care of our son. I was spoiled rotten. I guess one day he had really had enough and we got into this big argument about me not wanting to do anything.

He got really angry and began to curse at me and called me everything but a child of God. I thought that I was the one who was wrong because I was just being lazy so I accepted that the treatment that I was getting was warranted because it was all my fault. (That was my way of thinking at the time, but I know now that abuse, verbal or otherwise, is never acceptable.)

We never had a problem getting a babysitter when we wanted to go out. Most of the time his mother or his sister would babysit for us. Sometimes my sister would do it, but not very often. There were times that we would take the baby downtown to his mother's house and come back uptown to the house to hang out and have a good time together. We just needed some space and a little reprieve. We were new parents and raising a child was totally new to us. We loved our son, but we had started so early.

I started buying the Chief newspaper and applying for jobs. If I was working, then I would have just as much responsibility as he did and maybe that would be the solution to our arguing so much about the apartment and my not being more responsible in making our home his castle. Pure and simple, I was just plain lazy.

Thinking back to when I was growing up, it was not unusual for my friends to come to my house and call me to come outside to hang out. That is what we usually did. One weekend, my sister and I were doing our chores, like we usually had to do on the weekends. Since she knew that I really didn't like to clean much, she would take the living room, the bedroom, and the kitchen.

She would give me the hallway, the bathroom, and the dining room. I would give her such a hard time about doing my part, that one day she got so angry with me that she threw me out of the house in my pajamas and with my hair undone. My two friends came upstairs to call for me that day to come outside and here I was sitting in the hallway crying. I was so embarrassed. "My sister threw me out of the house and locked me out. My mother is downstairs doing the laundry could y'all please go down there and tell her what happened?" They did what I had asked of them and when my mother came home and let me in, it was me that got the whipping!

> **Golden Nugget:** **Ladies, keep a clean house. Not just for your spouse, but for yourself as well! Cleanliness is next to godliness. You never know when you might have an unexpected guest, and Jesus is omnipresent!**

I had applied for many different jobs and gone on many interviews. There was a lady in my building that I had heard would babysit children so I went to see her. She agreed to babysit for me if I got a job and she would watch my son when I went to interviews. Her apartment was always immaculate and she was a religious person. I found out later that she was a Jehovah's Witness, but she took great care of my son!

I finally got a job working at the Bronx VA. It was right up the hill from where I lived, only about two or three stops on the bus. I could even walk up the hill on a nice day and get some exercise.

I was hired as a file clerk in the Psychiatry Unit, but the position was only temporary. I did my job well and was trained by a wonderful woman. I remember that she loved to talk to me about Jesus and she was always so happy! Now that I had a job, things were a little better on the home front. We began to do the housework together. Whoever got home first would start dinner, and we would do the food shopping, cooking, and laundry together. Things were looking up! The only thing that didn't seem to change was his drinking habits and coming home most nights late from work. In the back of my mind, I began to think that maybe he was cheating on me.

Because of his behavior, most of our arguments were about him not spending time with me. After the argument, the making up part seemed to keep me quiet for a little while. The only thing wrong with that was I would get pregnant if he even looked at me too hard! Before I knew it, I had missed my period again. This time it was confirmed through a store-bought pregnancy test. I made the appointment with the doctor and he said that I was about six weeks. We decided that we just couldn't bring another baby into our relationship at this time. Our son was only two and a half years old and we weren't getting along so great. He went with me for the appointment, and when we left, we both cried.

Both of us were feeling guilty about the decision that we had made, but we couldn't turn back the hands of time. What was done was done and it was time to move on. It was so difficult though. Instead of that situation bringing us closer together, we began to drift further apart.

Since I felt in my heart that he was cheating on me, I began to flirt a little bit with this guy at my job that was giving me the attention that I wasn't getting at home. I began to rationalize it by saying to myself, "Well, we're not married. There's no ring on my finger." I had made many suggestions and hints about marriage, but his mind seemed to be far from it. I had always said that I wanted all my children to be from the same man. I felt so bad in my heart that my siblings and I all had different fathers. What was my mother thinking? I would never be in that boat, but I loved her and them just the same. We had been together for two years before we had our son, and he was already two and a half years old. It was time for him to put a ring on it. Shucks, I should have had the ring before the baby, but it was what it was. Somehow, getting married and having papers seemed like too much of a commitment for him and this just added more fuel to the fire. Adding this kind of pressure wasn't helping the situation, so we continued to live our lives together, but apart.

Have you ever been with someone, lived in the same place with the person and still felt lonely?

We did what we had to do in order to keep our family together and provide for our son but it wasn't easy. Since we had started out so early, we felt like we were missing that part of our life where we could hang out and have a good time. Don't get me wrong, we went places and did things together as a family, but something was still missing. We would get frustrated and argue a lot, but then we would make up and everything would be alright, at least for a little while.

The time went by pretty fast, and a spot opened up at my job that gave me the opportunity to become a permanent employee. It felt so good to know that I now had some security in my federal job and could not just be fired on a whim. My boyfriend was also moving up very quickly in the car business where he worked. He brought home good money and he was the perfect provider. He loved to go food shopping and sometimes we would go to three or four different stores just to get the sales. We would always check the circulars first so we would know which store had what. I guess things weren't all that bad... yet.

Since our son was older now, he was able to go to nursery school. I was so grateful to get him into the school and I became an active parent there. His babysitter would pick him up for me and keep him until I came home from work until they started staying open until 6pm, and then I would usually pick him up when I got off from work. Time flew by and when our son was about three years old, I found out I was pregnant again. I just couldn't put myself through another abortion, so we decided to have the baby.

I remember in November of 1984 when I was about five months along, we were downtown at his house for Thanksgiving. I had eaten so much food that it didn't make sense. I was so full! I got up to go to the restroom and discovered that I was bleeding. My God, I shouldn't be bleeding, I was pregnant! Right away I thought that I was having a miscarriage.

I told him what was happening and we got in a cab and rushed to the hospital. The doctor examined me and explained to us that I had something called Placenta Previa. Apparently, the placenta was covering the baby's head and if she moved a certain way against it, it would cause the bleeding. The doctor informed us that it was a possibility that the baby could turn around and change position and everything would be alright, but if not, I might need to have a C-section. I was quite dismayed about possibly having a C-section, but at least I knew in advance that it was a possibility and I just wanted a healthy baby!

Instead of things getting better at this point, with another baby on the way, they seemed to get worse. Now I really had an excuse not to do too much housework and I wasn't really able to fulfill his desires as much now because of the problems that I was having with this pregnancy. He was afraid that it would make me bleed and hurt the baby, so we refrained. That put a strain on our relationship, but nevertheless, we tried to stick it out.

In December of that year, I wound up having to stay in the hospital because of my condition. I was in the hospital on bed rest on New Year's Eve. Even though I was in the hospital, when that ball dropped I was walking around in the hallway shouting, "Happy New Year!" The nurse then reminded me that I was in the hospital and people were trying to rest. I thought that was the least I could do since I couldn't be home smoking weed and having champagne like I would normally do for New Year's Eve. I was quite disappointed that nobody wanted to celebrate with me, so I took my pregnant self to bed.

The next day when the doctor came to see me, I asked him if he knew when I might be released from the hospital. He replied, "That's what's wrong with y'all, you come in here for bed rest and then before you know it your baby comes out dead!" What the what?! I could not believe that this man said that to me! He must have been upset that he had to work on New Year's Day after he probably partied the night before and had to come to work with his hangover. Clearly, that is what must have been wrong with him for him to talk to me like that!

Later that day, when my boyfriend came to see me, I told him what the doctor had said. At first, I wasn't going to tell him because I knew that he had somewhat of a temper and I did not want him to haul off and punch the doctor in the mouth. Actually, I was surprised at what he did after I told him. He stated that he did not want to even see the doctor because he did not want to take any chances and get into a physical altercation with him because "that's what they expect us to do." He went straight to the nurse's station and asked for the doctor's supervisor. It felt good to see him handle this situation in such a diplomatic way. It was later that day or the next day that they released me and I went home.

My baby brother's birthday was on February 3rd and we gave him a party. Our apartment was pretty empty because we were getting new furniture and we were having the apartment painted first. We had a good time with plenty of food, drinks, music, and dancing! After everyone left, I spent some time in the kitchen taking the canned goods down out of the cabinets and packing them away to get ready for the painters. Not too long after that, we all went to bed. I got up in the middle of the night to use the bathroom and discovered I was bleeding again. This time it was so heavy that I couldn't even get up off the stool. I tried to call to my boyfriend from the bathroom but he was asleep. I yelled for him at the top of my lungs and finally, he got up and came to see about me. I told him what was going on and we called my sister to come over and watch our son while we took a cab to the hospital. I remember the inside lining of my coat being full of blood. When I felt the baby move when we were in the cab, I was so grateful because I thought that I was losing her. When we arrived at the hospital, they took me in immediately and hooked me up to the machines. When I heard her heartbeat and felt her moving, I was a little more at ease. They allowed me to just stay there because I was actually having contractions at that time and they wanted to see if she would turn around for a regular delivery. Unfortunately, she did not turn around and I wound up having to have the C-section. Back then, they did not allow the father to come into the delivery room during a C-section.

A few weeks before I was going to deliver, I heard a story on the news where a lady stole a baby from the same hospital that I was now having my baby in. I told her father that he better make sure he was standing outside the delivery room when they brought her out, make sure she has her tags on with my name on them, and follow her to the nursery to make sure that she is safe! Huh! I wasn't playing no games with those people!

We now had two children to care for. It didn't seem to make things any easier at all... instead, it became more difficult. He wasn't as involved with our daughter as he was with our son because he said that it was "hard for him to clean her good," so changing diapers was always my job. Sometimes he would get up in the middle of the night for feedings, but usually only on the weekends since he had to get up for work during the week. He had to get up really early, around 5am or so, but he was used to it because even on the weekends he was up at that time.

I took about three months off from my job for maternity leave and while the disability payments that I was receiving while on maternity leave weren't much, we were making it. It was a little more pressure on him now so the arguments increased and the drinking and late nights became more frequent.

A few months after the birth of my daughter, I began searching for my father again. It seemed like a losing battle since I didn't really have too much information on him and this time I didn't put as much into it as I had the first time. I became easily discouraged and gave up trying.

Before I left on my maternity leave, my employer was promising to give me a promotion to a GS-12 since I was only a GS-10. We could use the extra money since we now had another mouth to feed. I was now a secretary for the Chief of MIS (Medical Information Services) and I did my job well! I was very detail oriented and very professional. What I did at home was my business. As long as I did what I was supposed to do at work, that was all that mattered. When I was out of work taking care of my son, I had put in quite a few applications for jobs. I received some results in the mail for a test that I had taken for the police department as a PAA (Police Administrative Aide). I had aced it with flying colors and I was so happy! I knew that it wouldn't be long before they sent me the paperwork to come in for an interview. When I received the paperwork, I didn't tell anyone at my job. I was just planning to give them their two weeks' notice and be out. I thought that since they kept hemming and hawing about my promotion they didn't deserve to know. I aced the interview and received the paperwork in the mail with my start date. When I gave my supervisor my letter of resignation and two weeks' notice that I would be leaving, she said, "Oh, we just put in the paperwork for you to get your GS-12." I told them that they could keep that GS-12 because I was about to get a $10,000-dollar promotion with the NYPD! Bye!!!

Chapter 4

THE DOWNWARD SPIRAL

In order to start my job as a PAA with the police department, I had to attend the police academy first. We had to attend regular classes as if we were back in school again (which we were, sort of). There was so much information to learn about the job for which we had been hired.

It was always easy for me to make friends in life. Even when I was younger, I would be the girl who came up to you and said, "Hi, my name is Tracey. What's your name? You wanna play?" It was just easy for me. This was no different. I became acquainted with at least two young ladies, and we always went to lunch together and even began to hang out together sometimes on the weekends. We became pretty close and wound up working at the same precinct.

Being the new kid on the block, of course, I was stuck on the midnight shift. In a way, it was good for me because the shift was from 11pm to 7am. When I left the house, the kids were asleep and when I came home, I got them up, got them ready for school and the babysitter and went back home to try to get some sleep. It was kind of difficult because it was hard to sleep during the day. The sun was out and it seemed like they would always do repairs or construction with a drill in the neighborhood while I was trying to sleep. Before I knew it, it would be time to pick up the kids, start dinner and try to get maybe an hour of sleep before it was time to go to work.

I worked in the Complaint Room, which was exactly what it sounded like. It's the room where everyone came to file their complaints. The job itself was pretty easy, mostly just putting information into the computer. It was dealing with people that was sometimes the difficult part. I had to take reports for domestic violence incidents, car accidents and much more. Between my home life and the job, things were really starting to weigh on me. I found myself getting high a little bit more to try and shut things out temporarily, but when the high wore off, all of the problems were still there. I know that you're probably thinking, "What? She was still getting high and she worked for the police department?" Yep! The enemy had a hold on me and this was just the beginning... it gets worse.

One of my friends began to date this guy who sold cocaine. It was only on occasion when we would go out to party that we would sometimes use it. Slowly but surely, addiction got hold of me and I began to do it more frequently, even when I wasn't going out to a party. Sometimes I would go to her house to hang out and she would have some blow and give me a taste. Then she would say, "Well, I can't give you any more, that was my personal. If you want anything else you have to buy it."

Before I knew it, I had spent so much money that it didn't make sense. The worst part was that the children's father and I were both using. Most of our arguments began over drugs, money or not spending enough quality time together. Things began to get much worse. He began to drink and hang out more and I became a functioning cocaine addict.

At first, I was still able to take care of my children and my household, pay my bills and take care of my responsibilities. What made it really difficult was that the dealer made it so easy for us to get it. We could call him up and he would come and deliver it to us. Sometimes, we were even able to get it on credit. It was a good thing at the time when you wanted something and didn't have the money, but then when payday came and it was time to pay that bill, well, that was another story.

I don't know if any of you have ever sniffed cocaine before, but one of the side effects from it is that it keeps you up and wired, and it's usually hard to go right to sleep for a while. It also takes away your appetite for food. It has the opposite effect of weed, which makes you hungry and gives you the munchies. When you are sniffing, you don't have a desire to eat. That's why so many people who are addicted to cocaine lose weight.

When I used to get high, it also made my mouth twitch and I would talk funny. Blowing my nose a thousand times was a given. I sniffed so much cocaine that there was actually a hole in my nose where the membranes were just eaten away. Another side effect of cocaine was that it acted as an aphrodisiac. When I would sniff it would heighten my sexual desires. A few times, I gave in to these desires with one woman in particular. We would get high and then the next thing I know we were doing something that I never thought I would do. Was this really happening to me? It's been said that the flesh wants what it wants when it wants it.

The fact that I was having such a hard time in my relationship didn't help the situation. I couldn't remember the last time that we had been intimate.

The arguments between my boyfriend and I were so out of control that we now used to curse each other out, sometimes in front of the kids. It would hurt me so much when he would call me a "b" along with other names and I would, in turn, curse him out right back. One night, the argument was so bad and he was so angry. I was so scared that I woke up my daughter and held her because I knew if I had her in my arms, he wouldn't hit me. The house was really a mess now because I would always be so angry with him for something that he did or said that I had no desire to clean the house or do anything that made him happy. He, in turn, was so angry with me for not wanting to do anything that he made sure he didn't do anything that would make me happy. It went on like this for quite some time, and then I found out that I was pregnant again.

With what was currently going on in our relationship, I knew that I could not bring another child into our madness. This time I had to go on my own. After it was all said and done, while it still hurt, it didn't hurt as much as before, probably because of the situation and what we were experiencing in our relationship. Marriage was definitely out of the question at this point. We would keep breaking up and then getting back together. I would get mad at him and ask him for the house keys back. His name wasn't on the lease and I'm sure that me doing this to him every time I was angry with him made him really upset.

I didn't care though because usually when I did it, it was because of something he did that was disrespectful to me and I knew that by doing this it would make him angry. I wanted him to hurt just like I was hurting. When he would refuse to give me the keys back, I would wait for him to go to sleep, then take them and hide them from him so that he couldn't find them in the morning. We were both a piece of work!

The time came when I was finally able to come off the midnight shift. I was so happy about being able to work regular hours like a normal person. I went to work upstairs in the precinct in the Roll Call Unit. I was responsible for taking notifications and processing the roll calls using the Automated Roll Call System. It was very interesting, but it was a lot of work. I got to know most of the police officers a little better and one, in particular, began to spark my interest. Before I knew it, I was flirting and he was flirting back. I felt the desire to look for the attention that I was not receiving at home since I still didn't have a ring on my finger.

Years before, remember my friend that had asked me if I ever thought about what happens to us when we die? Well, we were still in touch and she started inviting me to her church. I always told her that I would come one day, but at the time I was still getting my head bad and I wasn't thinking about going to nobody's church! Now I started to think about it – maybe that was the change that I needed in my life. I called her and told her that I would go to church with her. She told me that she had to be there early and that I could just meet her there.

That Sunday, I kept my word and went to the church. When I walked into that church, I had never seen or felt anything like that before in my life! When I first entered, there was something going on and we had to stand in the back until it was finished before we could walk down the aisle. All of a sudden, I felt this tingling feeling and the hairs on the back of my neck seemed to stand straight up. I had never felt anything like this before in my life! What in the world was going on? During the service, the people were shouting and dancing and the choir was so good! It seemed like every song they sang ministered to my spirit and the words just had me in tears. When the Word was brought forth, I knew for sure that she had told this man all of my business and he must have known that I was going to be there that morning! I told myself that when I got ready to get myself together, this is where I was coming — I just didn't know at that time that I couldn't get myself together!

A few months later, they allowed me to go and work in the Summons Unit at work. The older Caucasian man that I worked with was really nice and trained me in my new responsibilities. In the Summons Unit, we were responsible for keeping an accurate count of the incoming summonses by processing them and distributing them to the appropriate agencies.

I started looking for my father again. One day in February of 1990, while I was at work, my co-worker was looking at the newspaper and he happened to come across an article about a young girl named Ricks who ran track. He knew that I was looking for my dad, so he gave it to me hoping that it would help.

I read the article and then I called the school that the girl attended and shared my situation with them. The person said that they would take my information and give it to the young lady to give to her parents, but that wasn't enough for me. I grabbed the Westchester telephone book, because that's where the school was, and I started looking under the last name Ricks. I came across a name that looked familiar to me from when I had cleaned out some of my mother's belongings.

When I dialed the number and the lady answered the phone, I proceeded to share my story with her. She said, "Tracey, your mother and father brought you to my house when you were a little itty-bitty girl!" I burst into tears — I had found the link! I know that it was the Lord that allowed this to take place because He knew that the place where I was in my life was not good. She gave me a telephone number for my father so that I could contact him. Since I had broken down so badly at work while just talking to her, I decided that I would wait until I got home before I called him — I had had enough embarrassment in the workplace for one day. Little did I know that she called him to let him know that she had spoken with me and he was expecting my call.

When I got home from work, I told the children's father what had happened. He was excited for me but suggested that I let him call first and speak to my dad because we didn't know how he was going to take it. I appreciated that because I don't know if I could have handled the rejection if it was going to go that way. He dialed the phone and when my dad answered he informed him that I was there and wanted to speak with him. I got on the phone and I cried! I had finally located my dad! We made arrangements for him to come over to my house to visit. I was so excited, but when the day came, I sat and waited, and waited, and soon I began to feel the rejection and disappointment that I had felt so many times before. Then the phone rang.

The heavy snowfall had caused a leak in the roof of his house and he was working on it to try and get it fixed. He thought he would be done in time but he wasn't. I understood but I was still disappointed. We set up another date for him to come over. While I was waiting for that day to arrive, I was still struggling with getting high. The day came and I finally got the chance to see my dad again! He was a short man, but he was nice looking like I remembered from before, just much older now. I shared with him what had happened with my mom and the fact that he now had two grandchildren. He told me that he had always told my mom that she could get in touch with him if she needed anything, but my mother was a strong, independent woman and she would not depend on a man for anything. She raised us all to the best of her ability and we never went hungry! At that point, I thought to myself, "Okay, but where was your desire to still see me and have a relationship with me even though you didn't hear from my mom?" I found out that he was a pastor (I know that this was a God thing) saved, sanctified and filled with the Holy Ghost, and that he only lived about 15 minutes away from me by car. He said that I had two brothers that lived with him and he had told them that they had a sister. Apparently, they went to the high school in my neighborhood and he wanted them to know that I existed, but I hadn't met them yet.

On March 2, 1990, I attended a service at his church. That's when we all met each other. I remember his wife talking to me about the Lord after service. She asked me if I had ever accepted the Lord Jesus Christ as my personal Savior. I told her that I had been to a church before and I told her about my experience, but I had never made a commitment to accept the Lord. Well, that day I did! She gave me a little green Bible and I wrote the date in the back – the date that I had made the choice to accept the Lord Jesus Christ as my personal Savior. My birthday was coming up and we had made plans to go out to dinner and celebrate. When my birthday came, I was reluctant to go because I had started getting high earlier on in the day and besides not having an appetite, I didn't want them to see me in that condition. I went anyway and we had a good time, although I'm sure that my stepmother knew and didn't say anything about it.

I was grateful that the Lord had allowed me to find my dad and have a relationship with him. His wife had told me that my father really wasn't a phone person so that if we didn't talk that much on the phone, it wasn't because he didn't love me – that's just the way he was. We started attending his church services, but I was still struggling with getting high. The Lord allowed me to have nine years with Dad and I was so grateful!

In December of 1999, the Lord called Dad home from labor to reward, and in July of 2010, the Lord called his wife home as well — my stepmother, the woman who had witnessed to me about the Lord when I received the Lord Jesus Christ as my personal Savior.

She shared the same birthday as my younger brother, and she went home to be with the Lord on the same day that my spiritual sister celebrates her birthday.

These are two dates that I will never forget. I thank and I praise God for the both of them and what we were able to share together.

On Valentine's Day of 1991, my boyfriend and I finally got married. We went to the Justice of the Peace because we were already living together and had been together for so many years and we had two children, so we didn't see the need to spend a whole lot of money on a big wedding. I was getting married even though I still wasn't sure if I was doing the right thing. One day during our breakup process, before we got married, he had moved out and gone to live in an apartment with his brother. The only problem with that was that he still had my house keys.

I found a paper in the house with his new address written on it. They were having a housewarming party and I wasn't invited. I was in the house getting high, and I believe that the kids were spending the night at their grandmother's house. I was so angry that I hopped in a cab and went to the address that was on the paper. I began ringing the bell and someone looked out the window, but no one would come to open the door. A cab pulled up in front of the house, but no one ever came outside.

At the time, I thought that maybe his girlfriend was up there and she was trying to leave until she realized that she would have to pass me in order to get into the cab. (That was just my thought process.) The lady who owned the house came out and asked me what was going on.

I told her that I needed to get in, to go upstairs and she said that if the people that I wanted to see weren't coming down to let me in then she couldn't let me in either. She went back inside and I kept ringing the bell. When my boyfriend came downstairs we got into a big argument and I told him that he needed to give me back my keys. He was no longer living in my apartment, so, therefore, he did not need to have my keys. Before I knew it, we were physically fighting. I don't know who threw the first punch, but at that point, it didn't even matter. When we finally stopped and I walked away, I felt something running down my face. When I touched it, I saw that it was blood. I went to the precinct to make a report but they told me that I had the wrong precinct and I needed to go to the one that covered that area. The next day, I had a "love mark" on my right eyelid and on the right side of my nose, but I married him anyway.

Before I knew it, I was pregnant again. When I was in my seventh month, I realized that I hadn't felt the baby move for a few days. I told my husband, and we went to the hospital, where they took me into the room and hooked me up to the machines. I remember the doctor having this "look" on his face and I knew that I had lost the baby. The doctor said that they weren't going to induce labor because when that happens, it usually sends a message to the uterus and I would go into labor on my own. I had to walk around for a whole week knowing that the baby inside of me was dead. That was so difficult. I didn't tell anybody, so the people in my building that would see me would say, "Hi Mommy!" and I would just cry. After the week was up and I did not go into labor, I went back to the hospital.

They induced me and I had to go through the contractions and give birth to something that had no life. After the little boy came out, they made us hold him and everything. They said it was a part of the grief process. I remember his dad holding him, sitting on the floor in the hallway and crying. When we left the hospital, they gave us a packet with pictures of him and papers with his hand and footprints. That was such a difficult thing to endure, and even though I didn't have a relationship with the Lord at that time, I knew that it could have only been Him who had brought me through!

I started attending the church intermittently now because I really needed the Lord Jesus Christ in my life, and at some point, I wound up getting baptized in Jesus' Name! I needed for all of my sins to be washed away because I was a hot mess! I always felt good when I went to church, but when I was home it was like I was in the same boat all over again. I knew that I needed the Holy Ghost and I felt that once I received it, it would change my life! I began to tarry for it, and when I didn't receive it right away, I got discouraged and thought that maybe since I had done so much bad in my life the Lord didn't want to give it to me.

We all know that the devil is a liar!

When I would go to the Upper Room and get on my knees, the enemy kept showing me myself sitting at the table getting high, or in a compromising position with someone, or just allowing me to see myself doing such ungodly things.

It wasn't until I became aware of the enemy's devices that I started picturing Jesus Christ hanging on that cross and shedding His blood for my sins every time I went down on my knees! The enemy had to give up because he could not get through the blood of Jesus!

I remember that night like it was yesterday. On September 22, 1991, a Sunday night, I was at the altar crying out to the Lord for the Holy Ghost until I was the last one there and they were about to close the church. The kids had gone somewhere with their father that weekend and I went home to an empty apartment. I was so determined to receive the Holy Ghost that I began tarrying again by myself in my living room. I felt the spirit of discouragement trying to come upon me, so I stopped and asked the Lord why I couldn't receive. He said to me, "If you tarry for one more hour, I will fill you!" That was about 1am.

Surely enough, about 2am or so on Monday, September 23, 1991, I began speaking in tongues as the Spirit of God gave the utterance! Oh, the joy that came to me when I knew that I was free! When my Savior found me, put His arms around me, oh the joy, great joy that came to me! I remember rolling on the floor speaking in tongues and laughing at the same time. It was late, but I wanted everyone to know that I had just received the Holy Ghost and I couldn't wait to tell somebody!

Later that morning, I left the apartment to go to the store. When I walked out of the building, I ran right into the same lady who had told me my mother didn't make it to Heaven. Of course, I had since forgiven her and at this point, I was ecstatic just to see her and share with her my good news! I just looked at her and she was able to see the glow of the Holy Ghost! She said to me, "You got it?!" and I said, "Yep! I got it!" We shouted right there on that sidewalk like there was no tomorrow!

I was so happy that I was trying to get everybody saved! After I was filled, praise God, I stopped wearing pants, stopped wearing makeup, stopped smoking cigarettes and I wanted everybody else that I was around to stop too! I remember being at work one day in the Roll Call Unit and everyone was able to see the change that had taken place in me. I began to complain about them smoking cigarettes in the office because now the smoke would bother me. My coworkers said, "Look, you found Jesus and that's wonderful, but you need to leave us alone." Here came the fight. I loved to go to church and I would have a wonderful time there, but when I got home it was a different story.

While we were trying to work things out, I found out I was pregnant again. I definitely wanted to keep this baby since I had just lost one. Things were going well and I was excited about this pregnancy. This would actually be a child of the marriage! I was trying really hard to do everything right but I wasn't gaining weight like I should have. I was grateful that the doctor told me that there was a good chance that I wouldn't have to have a C-section if everything went well. I was ecstatic at that news. I had heard "once a C-section always a C-section," but thank God, in this case, it wasn't so. When I gave birth to this beautiful baby boy, he was quite small, weighing only 4lbs.13oz.

I was so afraid that the doctor wouldn't let me take him home since he was not five pounds yet. I asked the doctor to please allow me to take my child home since I had left that same hospital not too long ago without my baby. He said that as long as his labs came back okay, I would be able to take him home, and I did! Thank God!

At this point, we were married but somehow it seemed to make things a little bit more difficult. The Bible says in **Amos 3:3, "Can two walk together, except they be agreed?"** It seemed like things were starting to get worse in my life instead of better. I was saved now so I didn't understand what the problem was, but the enemy had turned up the heat because he had lost me and wanted me back. I was trying to put up a good fight, but it just seemed like a losing battle. I had met this older woman in the church who lived in my neighborhood. We became friends and sometimes I would go to her house and we would read the Word together and spend time. She was my first spiritual mother and I shared with her about my past, including my drug addiction.

I remember sometimes on Friday nights I would go to service and have a wonderful time, but when I came home, my husband would be sitting at the dining room table getting high. Before I knew it, I had the bill in my hand and I would start to sniff too. But, how could this be? I was saved and filled with the Holy Ghost! I would start talking about the things of God while we were getting high. I remember him saying, "I don't want to talk about that while we're doing this."

I replied, "Yeah, I know but that just goes to show you how powerful He really is." I would repent and start over again.

One day I saw my spiritual mom and I was high. She knew it too! She said to me, "There is no sense playing with God. You may as well go back out there and do what you want to do. Don't go to hell through the church. Do what you want and go bust hell wide open." I was not ready for that. I was expecting her to talk to me and show me love and instead, she was rebuking me. I was a babe in Christ and I didn't know any better. I did not want to play with God like she said and so I went back into the world.

"Then goeth he, and taketh to him seven other spirits more wicked than himself;
and they enter in, and dwell there: and the last state of that man is worse than the first."
(Luke 11:26)

"For it had been better for them not to have known the way of righteousness, than, after they have known it, to turn from the holy commandment delivered unto them."
(2 Peter 2:21)

"Stand fast therefore in the liberty wherewith Christ hath made us free, and be not entangled again with the yoke of bondage."
(Galatians 5:1)

Before I knew it, the pants were back, the lipstick was back, the cigarettes, alcohol, and cocaine were back. I had put God to an open shame.

"If they shall fall away, to renew them again unto repentance; seeing they crucify to themselves the Son of God afresh, and put him to an open shame."
(Hebrews 6:6)

"So then because thou art lukewarm, and neither cold nor hot, I will spew thee out of my mouth."
(Revelation 3:16)

I had not fully submitted my will to the Will of God and now I was back at work where I had complained and they had seen the change in me. When I went back in the world, the old me resurfaced and they saw me doing everything that I had done before, so I'm sure that they thought that there was nothing to this Jesus thing. I was getting high so much and instead of being a functioning addict, I began to neglect my responsibilities and it was difficult to deal with life on life's terms. I was so embarrassed because of what I had done. Things really began to get worse now. I was dealing with seven more demons, each worse than the first. Our relationship wasn't getting any better and we were constantly breaking up and getting back together. We argued all the time. Most of the time it was because of the drugs or money.

I was so bad that I remember one night we were getting high. He said that he had had enough and was going to bed. Whatever he may have had left, he hid it from me. I finished what I had but then I wanted some more. He had hidden his stash on the top of the ceiling fan in the living room and I found it. The next day when it wasn't there, of course, there was another argument. I was definitely in the wrong for doing what I did, but I was so bound up that I didn't care.

I remember being at work and at lunchtime, I would go to the spot, buy my stuff, crush it up and get high. The devil really had me bound! It was no big deal for me to leave the house at 2am or 3am, just to go to the spot and get some more cocaine. I wasn't thinking about anybody bothering me. I wasn't frightened at all. I just wanted some more blow. Sometimes it was on a day when I had to get up and go to work, but I was wired. Around two in the afternoon, I would start to come down and it would be so difficult at that point to try to stay awake. Sometimes I would take a cab to go to the spot and the Spanish cab driver would be saved and listening to a Spanish Christian radio station. Hallelujah was the same in any language! I knew that the Lord was trying to get my attention. A lot of times I would see that truck that said GOD on the side. It really meant Guaranteed Overnight Delivery, but to me it meant GOD!!!

One day, I had just picked up some cocaine and I was on the bus going home to get my head bad! I went straight to the back and found a seat. A little while later, I heard someone say, "Praise the Lord, Tracey." When I looked up, I saw the sister who was the first person that I had seen after I had received the Holy Ghost. She was with her son. I said, "Oh, hi, Praise Him!" I wanted to crawl underneath the seat. I knew that the Lord had allowed this to happen because He was letting me know that He was still near. So many times, the Lord would allow me to run into the saints or pass by someone who would give me a tract. Sometimes it was really annoying, but sometimes it was really comforting to me because it was a reminder of where I really needed to be. I got way out of hand and found myself getting high almost every other day. I was out of control.

There was a time when I had bought an "8-ball," which is three and a half grams of cocaine. I must have been up for two days. The kids were with their dad at the time. I had sniffed so much cocaine and my heart was beating so fast that I thought I was going to have a heart attack. I remember being in the bathroom and I heard my mother's voice say, "That's enough Tracey." That's when I truly believed in my heart that she was in Heaven. I told myself that if she was in hell, she would be egging me on, not telling me to stop. I don't know what made me do this, but I looked in the mirror and was trying to make myself speak in tongues so that I could see if the Lord was still with me, but the Holy Ghost was long gone! I cried out to the Lord and asked Him to spare my life. I told Him that if He would just get me out of this one, that I wouldn't do it anymore. He brought me through that experience and I was probably good for about two weeks... maybe.

In November of 1992, I was promoted to Senior Police Administrative Aide. It was a wonderful time in my life and my grandmother came to my graduation! What a proud moment, walking across that stage and shaking the hand of the Police Commissioner. In January of 1995, I became the supervisor of the Complaint Room where I originally started working as a PAA. My only issue was that I was still getting high!

There were times when I would pick up my Bible and open it up "just to see what would happen." Most of the time when I did that, the Lord would allow me to turn right to **1 John 1:9, "If we confess our sins, he is faithful and just to forgive us our sins, and to cleanse us from all unrighteousness."**

One time specifically, I opened up the Word and **2 Corinthians 6:17-18** came right off the pages, **"Wherefore come out from among them, and be ye separate, saith the Lord, and touch not the unclean thing; and I will receive you, and will be a Father unto you, and ye shall be my sons and daughters, saith the Lord Almighty."**

During this time in my backslidden struggle, I was fighting with myself. My spirit really wanted God, but my flesh was weak. I was a mess, trying to stay undercover and getting myself involved in so many unnecessary and unhealthy relationships. I was looking for love in all the wrong places. The love of my life wanted me to love Him, but instead, I was searching for someone to love me. I should have already known that love wasn't just good sex. It goes far deeper than that. At this point, I was sick and tired of being sick and tired. I would do so many crazy things sometimes, just to get money to buy drugs. One time I stole $100 from my grandmother and tried to blame it on my younger brother. I'm not proud of that, but even after that, I kept getting high.

In April of 1995, things came to a head. One day after work, I walked into the drug spot to buy my stuff. When I went inside I was shocked to see one of the officers that I worked with sitting at the table in plain clothes. The guy didn't want to sell him anything because he didn't know him. When he saw me he said, "There goes my friend. Tracey, tell him that I'm okay please so that I can get my stuff." I wanted to die right there! I was petrified, but I couldn't let on just how scared I was. The guy was sitting there with the gun on the table. "Oh, he's okay," was my reply. The guy sold him the stuff and then looked at me and asked me what I wanted. I didn't want to buy anything at that point, but I didn't want to be the reason for us getting shot either, so I made my purchase and left. I went home and got high.

The next day, I had to go downtown for training, so I was not at work. I found out later that IAD (Internal Affairs Division) came to the job looking for me but I wasn't there. When I got home from the training about 4:45pm, I wasn't in the house for fifteen minutes when I heard a knock at the door. It was the police. I was so scared and I did not want to open the door for them, but after I thought about it, I figured that it was better to deal with it while my children weren't home so I opened the door. There were three men and one woman. They came in and my house was a mess. They told me that I needed to go with them to take a Dole test (Drug test). I needed to use the bathroom before we left and they sent the woman with me, I guess to make sure that I wasn't trying to get rid of anything, but I didn't have anything. (Thank God!)

When we were in the hallway, one of the men asked me if there was a back way out of my building because a lot of my nosy neighbors were sitting downstairs in front of the building and they didn't want them to see me. He said that they weren't going to cuff me or anything — I guess that they were trying to spare me the embarrassment of my neighbors seeing me with them. (Look at God, even in this!) We went out of the back way and they took me to a building on Fordham Road in the Bronx. The main detective told me, "You're such a nice lady, but you just have a bad problem, that's all." He said that I had so much cocaine in my system that it didn't make sense.

After all of this, I wound up losing my good city job but God was so good to me that I was allowed to resign with the permission of the Police Commissioner so that I would be able to get another city, state or federal job someday.

All at the same time, my grandmother died, I lost my good paying city job due to drugs and I was separated from my husband. My life had gone so far downhill and I didn't know what to do with myself. On Saturday night, September 23,

1995, (exactly four years after I first got saved and received the Holy Ghost) after my husband came to pick up the kids for the weekend, he gave me the child support money and almost as soon as they left, I left right behind them and made my way to the spot. That night I believe I picked up an "8 ball." I went home and I had everything that I needed. My blow, my cigarettes, my wine coolers, I was good. I got high all night long, by myself. Around 2am, I was watching "Saturday Night at the Apollo" on TV. All of a sudden, the Lord began to give me a poem about deliverance. I had been writing poetry since I was twelve years old. I turned down the TV and began to write. It was an awesome poem and I felt so convicted. It was so funny how the Lord was giving me the words to write, but it didn't feel like they were actually coming from me.

After I finished writing, the enemy said, "Don't forget that you still have some more blow in that bill. That stuff is expensive, don't let it go to waste. You still have some more wine coolers too." I listened to the enemy and turned the TV back up, finished my blow and my wine cooler... and felt horrible.

I fell to my knees and began to cry out to the Lord. I told Him that I didn't want to continue living my life this way. I told Him that I was a mess and that I was sorry for walking away from Him and for the things that I had done. I was truly repenting. When I was done, the Lord spoke to me as clear as day and said, "Go to church."

I didn't get to sleep until around 4am because I had so much cocaine in my system and I set my clock for 8am. When the clock went off, I turned it off and fell back to sleep. I did not hit the snooze button, I turned it OFF! At 8:30 the Lord woke me up and said, "I said go to church!" I tried to call my spiritual mother and was not able to get her on the phone. Then I tried to call the other sister who was the first one to hear that I had the Holy Ghost, but she didn't answer her phone either. At that point, the Lord said, "You don't need nobody else but me!" With that, I took my shower, got ready and left the house. When I got down to the church I sat upstairs in the balcony.

Our assistant pastor preached a message that morning titled "Backslider Come Home!" That message was definitely for me! Before I could even get to the altar for the altar call, I stood up and began to cry out to the Lord. Right then and there the Lord refilled me with the gift of the Holy Ghost speaking in tongues as the Spirit of God gives the utterance and from that day on I never touched drugs or cigarettes again! I thank and I praise God for my G.O.D.! **Guaranteed Overnight Delivery!**

Later that night, when I went to bed, the Lord gave me a dream. In the dream, I was all dressed up in this beautiful white dress. My hair was done and I was in a place that was grassy and had a whole lot of flowers. The sun was shining bright and I was just frolicking in the area having a wonderful time. All of a sudden, I tripped and fell. I lost my footing and began rolling down the side of a hill. When I reached the bottom, it was dirty and muddy, and my dress got filthy, my hair had mud in it and I was saying, "Oh my God, how did I get down here? No! I don't want to stay down here… I want to go back up there!" As I began to try to climb my way back up the hill, every single rock that I would grab hold of crumbled underneath my hands and I couldn't get back up. I began to cry uncontrollably and then the Lord woke me up. I knew in my heart that the Lord was letting me know that if I left Him again, I might not make it back. But it didn't end there…

Dad with me at five months old.

They called me Rashy Ashy Tracey (the rash around my mouth).

An Easter outfit Mom made.

My 18th birthday in a dress Mom made.

On my way to the Poconos.

Prom picture in a dress Mom made.

High School graduation with Nana and Mommy.

My sick Mommy, Nana, my brother, my son as a baby and me.

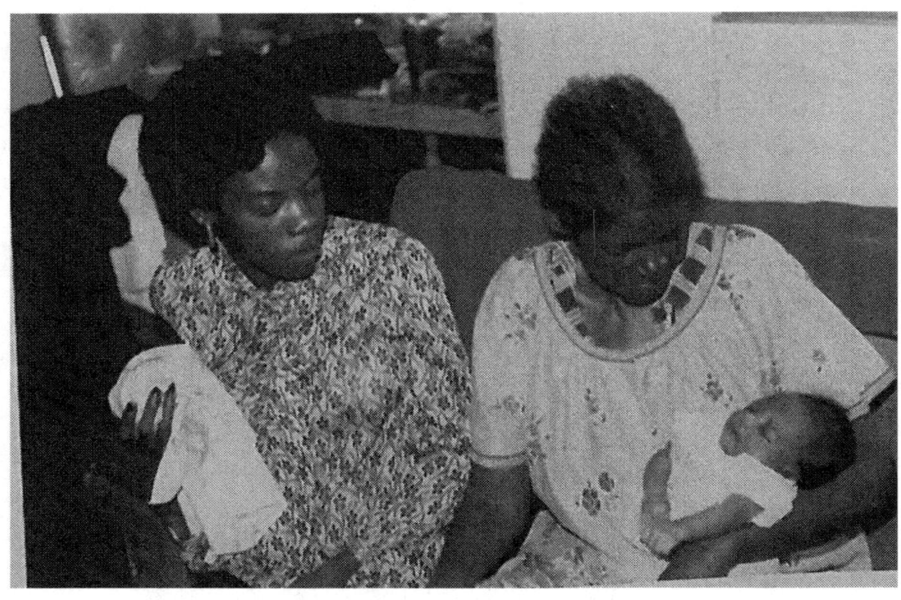

Me with Mom holding her first grandchild, my son.

Reunited with Dad!

Celebrating my birthday with Dad.

Saved and starting life anew!

Chapter 5

THE UPHILL BATTLE

Now that the Lord had refilled me with the Holy Ghost, I was truly singing the song, "I'm running for my life, I'm running for my life, I'm running for my life, I'm running for my life, if anybody asks you, what's the matter with me, just tell them I'm saved, sanctified, Holy Ghost filled and fire baptized, I got Jesus on my side and I'm running for my life!" That was the truth and nothing but the truth! My children were fourteen, ten and three years old at this time. I was so grateful for what the Lord had done for me that I was in church most of the time. Almost every time the doors opened you could find me in the House of God! It was good for my spirit, but not for my family. I didn't know this at the time. I just thought that I really needed to be there as much as possible, because I did not want to go anywhere near the life that I had been living.

> **Golden Nugget:** Ladies and Gents, the proper order is Jesus, spouse, children, church. So many times, we put the church first and we neglect to take care of our homes, spouses or children. Mothers, please do not keep your children out all night at church when there is school the next day. Gentlemen, if the Lord has given you a wife and children, please don't put the church before them. Especially if your spouse is not saved yet. I really learned this the hard way! Everything in decency and in order.

I was able to get my children active in the church in order to keep them busy and interested in coming. My older son was on the children's usher board, my daughter went to children's church and I would sometimes take the baby to the nursery during service so that I could be free to praise the Lord and enjoy the service. Sometimes my husband would come and sometimes he wouldn't. I began praying about what auxiliary to join in the church. I wanted to be doing something after I had completed my doctrine classes and had taken the right hand of fellowship. I needed to pray about it because I wanted to be where the Lord wanted me to be, not just joining something because someone was asking me to come and be a part of their group. What was Jesus saying?

I went to bed one night and the Lord gave me a dream. In the dream, I was in the house and the telephone rang. I picked up the phone and said, "Praise the Lord!" (like I do in real life) and the person on the other end said, "Oh Praise the Lord Sister Tracey! Wow! I didn't know that you answered your phone like that!"

I said, "Yes, I do all the time. How are you doing?"

"I am blessed, thank God," she said.

She then proceeded to invite me to a meeting that was coming up. She was the president of the group. I told her that I would attend and we hung up the phone. Then I woke up. After I woke up, I went into prayer. During prayer, the Lord gave me a Scripture. When I turned to it in the Word of God, it confirmed that this was the group I was supposed to join.

The following Sunday the group was having a meeting, which I attended. The president asked me why I wanted to be in that group and I told her about my dream. The Holy Ghost had given her confirmation as well and it was a blessing to be a part of something in the church! The group that the Lord had led me to was similar to a Junior Missionary group. They led devotions, worked with the souls at the altar, assisted in the Baptism Room and the Upper Room and also participated in outreach endeavors, such as going out to the nursing home. In order to be a part of this very spiritual auxiliary, you had to attend five meetings consecutively and attend one all night prayer session.

The young women in this group were very prayerful and we had a spiritual mother who was over the group who did not play. She was one of those praying mothers whose spiritual discernment was so on point! Sometimes the Lord would come in and take over our meetings and we would just allow Him to have His way. We prayed and fasted and I began to grow closer to the Lord and stronger in Him.

I was still having some problems in my marriage, but I knew that the Lord would help me. Sometimes, I would talk to different saints about some of the things that I was going through at home. "Daughter, you have to pray and fast. Turn your plate down. The sanctified wife will sanctify the husband. Don't worry, it will be alright!" That was wonderful advice, but they didn't live in my home. I was trying as much as possible to try to live holy and be that wife and mother that the Lord would have me to be, but it was so difficult at times.

There were nights when my husband would come home drunk and I would refuse to be intimate with him. Some of you might say that I was wrong to withhold from my husband, but you weren't in my home either. When he wasn't drinking or getting high, he was a wonderful provider and father. I was in the church, I was saved and filled with the Holy Ghost, but the Lord was still working on me.

One night, we got into this big argument. I don't remember now what it was even about. I do remember that he cursed me and called me everything in the book. It seemed to make him even angrier when I didn't fight back or argue with him. The day after the argument, he had a function to attend with the Boy Scouts and he was getting an award. I had told him that I wouldn't be attending because they were having it in the basement of a church and they were going to be serving liquor. How do you serve liquor inside of the church? I told him, "No, I'm not going, absolutely not!"

He had expressed to me a few days before that he didn't have anything nice to wear to this event. I had already purchased his Father's Day gifts and had put them away in the house. I had brought him three pairs of pants, three shirts and three ties for his gift. When I left in the morning, I took one of the outfits out and laid it out nicely on the couch for him since I knew that I would not be back before he left to go to the event. Before I could even make it out of the train station when I had reached my destination, my beeper was going off, with the house number on it. When I called him, he was almost in tears, apologizing to me for what had happened the night before and thanking me for what I had done.

At that point, I knew without a shadow of a doubt that I had the Holy Ghost for real, for real!

The Lord had really blessed me and I became gainfully employed as a security guard. I had on my light blue shirt and tie with a blue skirt. I did not wear pants and it was okay with them. It seemed like I was beginning my life over again. In the past, I would have never worked as a security guard because it seemed to me to be such a menial job, but I was grateful to just have a job after what I had gone through.

I stayed on that job for about two years, and when I was unemployed I was taking so many exams for state, city, and federal jobs. I received an employment inquiry from a work release correctional facility in the Bronx. I was so excited that I wore my blue and bone uniform that we used to serve in, to the interview. I was interviewed by an African American man who was the superintendent of the facility. During the interview, he looked at my resume and saw that a lot of time had passed since I had been released from the police department.

He said, "I see here that you worked for the police department for almost ten years. What happened?"

I said, "Well, sir, in that time of my life I was struggling with drug addiction. But I have since tapped into the spiritual side of my life and I refuse to allow mistakes that I have made in my past stop me from accomplishing the goals that I have set forth for my future!" He looked up at me with this huge smile on his face and I knew already that the Lord had blessed me and I had landed that job.

He said, "Okay, well, we have a few more interviews to do, but either way you will be hearing from us when we make a decision."

I said, "Okay, then, thank you so much for your time and you have a good day!"

When I walked out of that office, I knew that the job was mine. The very next day I received a call from the lady in Personnel and I was given my date to start. It is so on time the way that the Lord does things! I had previously worked at the VA Hospital and for the police department, and this job that I had been offered at the correctional facility was going to allow me to work in the medical unit. I felt that the Lord had already prepared me for this position with the previous jobs that I had held. This job was not easy though.

I was working in the medical unit with a nurse who had so much book sense that she had limited common sense. Apparently, she liked one of the counselors that worked there and I didn't know it. I was just being cordial to him like I was to everyone. She thought that I liked him and was trying to steal him from her and so she tried to make my life a living hell. She did everything that she could to get me to snap. She would talk nasty to me, try to write me up for no reason... all sorts of things. The administration liked me and the Lord had granted me favor with them. They knew what was going on with her and the Deputy of Security would always tell me, "I know that she's crazy. I can get you out of there if you want, just let me know." I told him that I needed to pray about it because I didn't want to move ahead of God.

I had shared my frustrations with my son's godmother, (the one who invited me to church long ago) and she shared her testimony with me about a similar situation that she had gone through. The end result was that the Lord moved the person and gave her the victory.

While I was praying about it, I was still putting in papers for a transfer or a promotion. I was called to the State Farm Insurance Company for an interview. I went to the interview and the lady wanted to hire me on the spot. Earlier that morning, before I went to the interview I was watching a TV evangelist. He was saying that when the enemy comes to try you, you have to stand. The lady that interviewed me walked out of the room and I heard the Holy Ghost say, "You have to stand!" When she came back in the room, I told her that I could not take the position. She asked me why not and I told her that sometimes you have to look at the whole picture and how it would affect everyone involved. She said that she understood and had me fill out the declination paper. She wouldn't have understood if I told her that the Lord would not let me do it.

When I left the office and went outside, a guy was walking towards me wearing a white t-shirt and on the front of it in different color letters it said, "STAND." I knew that was the Lord confirming His Word to me. About a week later, I found out that the nurse was going to be leaving the correctional facility. She had taken a position at the State Farm Insurance Company! If I had not listened and been obedient to the voice of the Lord, she could have ended up being my supervisor again!

It is a blessing to be able to hear the voice of the Lord when He speaks to you and then be obedient to the instructions that He gives. I hope that helped somebody right there! The Deputy of Security asked me what I did to get rid of her. I told him that all I did was pray and the Lord did the rest!

"Trust in the Lord with all thine heart; and lean not unto thine own understanding, in all thy ways acknowledge him and he shall direct thy paths." (Proverbs 3:5-6)

Sometimes my husband would come to church with me and the children. What an awesome thing for all of us to go to church together and fellowship! I loved those times! We still had disagreements, but things seemed to be looking up. I had been in the church for quite some time now and I had made friends. Never get too comfortable in your salvation because **1 Peter 5:8** says, **"Be sober, be vigilant, because your adversary the devil, as a roaring lion, walketh about, seeking whom he may devour."** How true is this Scripture! After a couple of years, we began to drift apart again because I was so into the church and I was not so much into my husband anymore. I would get frustrated because he would not come to church and we were walking two separate ways.

Instead of showing my husband love, I was condemning him to hell because of what he was doing. Before I knew it, I found myself searching for love outside of my marriage again. This time I found it in self-gratification and eventually with one of the other sisters in the church. I knew that it was wrong and I was so ashamed of myself.

I began to make friends with other females and when I did, the one that I was seeing would get very angry and jealous. One of the sisters said, "What's wrong with your friend? Why is she always angry with me? She doesn't even know me."

I tried to shrug it off, but it just got worse. Finally, I broke down and shared with this sister why I thought that she was being treated this way. I shared this with her in confidence, but unfortunately, she took my business and shared it with someone else and before I knew it, it was all over the church. The saints began to talk about me and shun me. I felt horrible and didn't know what to do. We had a revival in church and one night my husband came. He enjoyed the service and the preacher that brought forth the Word. Afterwards, he said, "Where is his church? I would love to go and visit there." It just so happens that his church was a small church and that was what my husband preferred. Thank you, Jesus! Now I had a way out! After a couple of visits to this other church, we decided that we would start attending there together. It was the perfect opportunity for me to run.

I spoke with our assistant pastor and told him that I was being led to attend the other church with my husband. He expressed his dismay about me leaving but told me that if for whatever reason things didn't work out, I was more than welcome to come back home at any time. I considered it a blessing that he left the door open for me if need be. We began attending the new church and it was good but different. There was no huge choir like back home, but the pastor was anointed to preach.

Sometimes the Holy Ghost would move in such a way that he would make the altar call before he even began to preach. My husband started tarrying for the Holy Ghost and would help out around the church. He began to get a little discouraged when he did not receive the Holy Ghost right away, and then things began to get a little bad again.

The arguments and disagreements began to come back again and so we committed to counseling with the pastor to try and save our marriage. The sessions seemed to be going well and I thought that we were making progress. Then here came the enemy and convinced my husband to do a 180 degree turn around. He wound up leaving the church and after a while, he and I separated again. I continued to go to counseling on my own because I needed the help and peace of mind. There were times when I would receive compliments from the pastor about my hair, or the way I was dressed. It was nice to hear these things, but I wasn't sure if they were just compliments or not. Then he started telling me that he loved me. I shrugged it off as him just being nice and that he loved me like a pastor loves a daughter. Until one day when he wound up in my house and my foot almost slipped!

What did I do next? What I knew how to do best — I ran again! It was time to go back home. I stopped attending that church and went back to my home church. I spoke with the assistant pastor and he welcomed me back with open arms. When he asked me what happened, I told him that my son was growing up and getting older (which he was) and the other church did not provide an outlet for him like ours did with the young adult usher board and children's church, so we came back home. It was a good thing that we did. I went back to the auxiliary that I was on before and after I completed the requirements, I began serving and being active again. It was a little difficult keeping my head up, but I had made up in my mind that regardless of whatever people were saying and doing, I was coming to church to serve my Lord and Savior Jesus Christ and not the people. Even after I had come back to my home church, it was very difficult for me to receive the Word from this man of God when he would come to my church to preach. I really had to pray and ask the Lord to help me and being the God that He is, He did!

One day, after I had returned to my home church, I was approached by the wife of one of our assistant pastors. While I was away, she started a group of young girls, something like a mentoring group, and for personal reasons, she was unable to continue leading it. She said that the Lord had put me in her spirit to take it over. I prayed about it and the Lord confirmed that I was to do it. I took over the group and I would discuss topics with them that they wouldn't get answers for during the Sunday morning service. We would discuss the Word, celebrate birthdays and have a good time.

One of the young boys was interested in one of our girls and inquired as to why the boys couldn't be a part of our group. I talked it over with the young ladies to see how they felt about it, and of course, I sought the Lord about now opening up the group to the young men as well. The Lord gave me clearance and the girls were in agreement, so we put "Sistah Talk" to rest and "Teen Talk" was born!

The group grew tremendously over the years and many of our teens were baptized and received the gift of the Holy Ghost. I remained the Teen Talk Coordinator for eleven years until the Lord released me. I was able to relate so well to the young people and shared so many of my testimonies with them about what I went through growing up. I always tried to give it to them real because the enemy is not playing with our youth! I still love all of them till this day. Most of them are grown now and have gone on with their lives, but I am hopeful that what was instilled and imparted to them will last them a lifetime!

Sometime after we had come back, my daughter was singing in one of the youth choirs. All of my children were active in the church and we were doing well. On October 31st, my daughter went down and got baptized in Jesus' Name! She began to tarry for the Holy Ghost and was filled not too long after one night at a youth service in the church. Now both of us were saved and filled! There were times when I would go up to the Upper Room to pray before service, and when I got there, she was already up there on her knees! One can chase a thousand, but two can put ten thousand to flight!

Before I knew it, my oldest son was graduating from high school and going off to college, my husband was back home and we were trying to work things out. Unfortunately, things were still so difficult. I kept hearing about how God didn't like divorce, but I was at my wit's end. I was fasting and praying and seeking God for answers but all I kept hearing was the voices of the saints. I tried to hold on and trust and believe the Lord for my marriage.

By the time I turned around again, my daughter was graduating high school and was on her way to college down south. It was quite disheartening to me when my daughter came home from high school one day with a hickey on her neck. All of her life she was very active in sports. She ran track, excelled in the high jump and relay races, she did karate and she played basketball, and was good at it too! I always supported her and would attend her track events, karate matches, and basketball games. When I saw the hickey on her neck and I asked her about it, I was floored when she told me that another girl put it there. When I first found out about my daughter's decision to live this life, I was heartbroken. I didn't want to look at her or speak to her. I didn't even think about what I had already been in myself. Did I bring that spirit into my home and now it was attacking my child? I really had to pray and seek the face of God. In prayer, the Lord spoke to me ever so sweetly and He said, "With loving kindness have I drawn thee. You've got to love her back to Me!" and that is exactly what I have been doing ever since!

In 2005, I went on a weekend trip with my sister in Christ from my new job. It was funny how we met. When she saw me, she asked me if I was saved. I'm quite sure that she looked at my outward appearance and somehow came to that conclusion. I said yes, I was, but at the time I didn't think that she was. Why? Because I was judging her from her outward appearance. Little did I know that she was saved, sanctified, Holy Ghost filled and fire baptized! We became the best of friends and it was such a blessing to have a saved sister in Christ on the job along with me!

A lot of times as saints, we tend to judge people by their outward appearance, but remember, the Word of God says that, **"man looketh on the outward appearance, but the Lord looketh on the heart" (1 Samuel 16:7).** Now, I'm not saying that as saints of God we should dress any old kind of way, please don't misunderstand me. We should adorn ourselves in "modest apparel that becometh holiness."

Oh, I forgot to tell y'all. I left the correctional facility and was offered a position at the Office of Children and Family Services, which I accepted. While I was there I was canvassed for a position with the Unified Court System as a Court Assistant. I had taken that test also when I was not working, and it was now coming through. I went on the interview and the Lord blessed me again and I aced it. When I did not receive a call after about a week, I called to follow up. I was informed that although my interview was top notch, I was unable to be reached on the list. "Just hang on, we will more than likely be calling you back real soon!" I was a little disappointed but I knew that God had a plan. We have to trust that God's timing is perfect. During this time, there were some summer youth workers that had come to our job. The Lord blessed me to befriend one of the young ladies and witness to her. She wound up coming to the church and getting baptized in Jesus' Name! About a week later, I was called back for the position and I accepted. Another $10,000 raise! I believe that's why the Lord held me back because He was sending someone for me to witness to!

I started that job in June of 2003. In 2005, when we went on the weekend trip, I had honestly prayed and told the Lord that I needed to hear directly from Him concerning this divorce thing. While at the Sexual Brokenness conference, I attended a one-on-one session with a woman that I had never seen before in my life. She shared some things with me that only the Lord knew. I felt like there was definitely purpose in my being there. After my one-on-one consultation, I went back to the room and I told the Lord, "God, you said, 'What God has joined together let no man put asunder.'" The Lord said to me, "I didn't put that marriage together... you did!" — and He was absolutely right!

When I got back home the usual things were happening. One night my husband came home around 5:00 in the morning. He went to the bathroom and then went straight to bed, knocked out cold. When I woke up in the morning, I went to the bathroom. As I was sitting there, the Holy Ghost told me to open the hamper. I was perplexed, but I was obedient and did as I was told. He showed me the evidence that I had been looking for regarding my husband's infidelity. That was the last straw and I filed for divorce. At the time, I didn't really tell too many people in the church that I was divorced because of the way that it is looked upon and frowned on. It wasn't until years later that I released it openly.

When my youngest son was in the tenth grade, my older son was already away at law school. He wanted my younger son to come and live with him, being that only the two of us were in the house. I guess that my older son felt that the younger one needed a positive male role model in his life. I told him that I would pray about it and I did. I honestly didn't want to let go, but the Lord gave me the okay to release him and to trust that He would still be there with them.

My older son became his legal guardian and in 2010 they both graduated – my older son from law school and my younger son from high school! Most of the family flew to where they were and we gave them a big party. Both of my sons were featured in an article in a magazine that was printed up by the law school, and what a grateful and proud momma I was! While we were there in my son's apartment, what was supposed to be a wonderful and happy occasion turned into one of my son's neighbors calling the cops because of a loud dispute between my ex-husband and me. It seemed like almost every time something good was taking place, something not so good wound up happening. Most of the time it was me getting cursed out and being disrespected due to the influence of the alcohol.

During this time, my daughter was in the service and was unable to attend. She had attended college for two years and then decided to go into the service like her older brother. We were there for her graduation and she received many awards. I was extremely proud of my baby girl! Now it was time to see my youngest son off to college – my, my, where was the time flying to? His uncle and I drove him up to his college and I took him shopping and fixed up his room before I left. You know how us mothers do! Now I had an empty nest since all of the children had gone, and I didn't know what to do with myself. I immersed myself in church, work and home.

My ex-husband and I still kept in touch after the divorce and became very good friends. One time, in particular, he needed a place to stay after he was released from rehab. I allowed him to come and stay in my apartment since I had two bedrooms and all of the kids were gone. He knew that he had to respect my home and he could not smoke cigarettes or have any alcohol or drugs in my house.

After about a month or so, I was at work one day. The Holy Ghost told me to leave work and go home. I wasn't sure why, but I was obedient to the Spirit of God and I left work early and went home. He was in the shower and didn't hear me put the key in the door. When I walked in the house, right there on the dining room table was a dollar bill with cocaine in it, and a bottle of liquor on the table and a beer in my refrigerator. That was the day he had to leave.

When I was home and alone, although I had the Lord and I had the Holy Ghost, sometimes my flesh got the better of me. Every now and then I would turn on the TV in the midnight hour and I would be left to myself. I had a silent struggle. Who would have thought that somewhere down the line I would wind up in another relationship with one of the sisters from the church again? I was afraid to leave the church because I knew that if I did, I would probably not make it back. I knew that this was totally wrong, as it goes against the Word of God as recorded in Romans 1:21-32 and Leviticus 18:22.

On Sunday, I would go to church and almost every time the Word would come forth, it would cut me like a knife. **Hebrews 4:12, "For the word of God is quick, and powerful, and sharper than any two-edged sword, piercing even to the dividing asunder of soul and spirit, and of the joints and marrow, and is a discerner of the thoughts and intents of the heart."** Here we go again. The rumors started flying, people started talking, it was being preached across the pulpit, folks didn't want to hug me anymore, the Lord was giving people dreams, mothers had discernment and then there were some who were praying for me. One sister would hug me and rebuke me at the same time as she would start pleading the blood. Why was I going through this trial again?

Romans 7: 22-23 says, **"For I delight in the law of God after the inward man: But I see another law in my members warring against the law of my mind, and bringing me into captivity to the law of sin which is in my members."**

For those that may not know, self-gratification is just another way that you open doors and allow the spirit of lesbianism and homosexuality to come upon you. So many are not aware of this fact and think that since they are not doing any harm by having a partner it's okay... but it's not.

Romans 12:1-2 says, **"I beseech you therefore, brethren, by the mercies of God that ye present your bodies a living sacrifice, holy, acceptable unto God, which is your reasonable service; and be not conformed to this world; but be ye transformed by the renewing of your mind, that ye may prove what is that good and acceptable, and perfect, will of God."**

"Because it is written, Be ye holy;
for I am holy."
(1 Peter 1:16)

Our God is a Holy God!

In August of 2013, my oldest son got married, and it was such a blessed event! The wedding was held in the state where the bride lived and most of my family and a few of my close friends flew in for the wedding.

I especially loved the part when the man of God showed us the meaning of the Unity Cross. The outside of it was plain white wood and it symbolized the man and how God had created the man first, as well as his strength and headship. There was a piece that fit inside of the first piece and it was curvy, beautiful and delicate. This second piece symbolized the woman, and how God made her from the rib in Adam's side, and she was beautiful and delicate and she complimented the man. He put the second piece inside of the first piece and put it on a black stand. The stand symbolized the Lord and that they both should stand upon Him and depend on Him. It also symbolized the fact that the Lord should be their solid foundation. I tell you, it made so much sense and it was so true!

It was such a blessing that my sister was able to attend the wedding! She kept saying that she wouldn't miss it for the world, and I am so grateful that she was able to have this experience because in September of that same year (2013), she passed away. I remember having a conversation with her concerning the fact that if my daughter was to marry another woman I would not attend the wedding. Our speaking about it turned into more of a debate but we ended the conversation with me telling her that it was the Will of God that all would come into the knowledge of salvation and be filled with the Holy Ghost. After we hung up that morning, I did not talk with her for two days. When I called her that morning of the third day, it went to her voicemail. I left her a message and my phone rang back from her number when I was in the shower, so I let it go to voicemail. When I called back, it was my niece. She was crying hysterically and said that my sister didn't seem to be breathing and EMS was there working on her. I told her that as soon as I walked the dog I would be on my way. As I was walking the dog back home my niece called me back to say that my sister didn't make it. I was devastated! I knew that she was having some medical issues, but nothing that I thought would cause her to leave us!

After Nana passed, she was the matriarch of our family. She would always try to bring us together for cookouts and during the holidays because we all had such busy lives and didn't see each other that often. I miss her so much!

<u>Golden Nugget</u>: Love your family! Spend time with them! Don't always try to beat them over the head with the Bible about Jesus. Witness to them about salvation however the Lord leads and then live the life in front of them. Tomorrow is not promised to any of us!

Even in the midst of my struggles, the Lord was still having mercy on my soul and I am grateful! In June of 2013, I had taken a promotional exam for my job for the third time. I had failed this same exam twice before. I requested a makeup date because, on the day that it was being given, I was going to be away at the Missionary Retreat. The Lord had given me favor and I was allowed to take the exam on that following Monday after I had returned. I studied very hard, and when I took the exam I felt like it could go either way, but I was determined to put my trust in God.

When I received the results by email in November of that year, I was so disappointed to learn that I had yet again failed this test! I was heartbroken. I vowed that this was going to be the last time that I was going to take that exam. My daughter, co-worker and sister in Christ all tried to encourage me, and I appreciated it. I finally threw up my hands and said, "Okay, Lord whatever you say! For we know that all things work together for good, to them that love the Lord, to those who are the called according to His purpose! Let Your Will be done!" I went on with my life and then on January 9, 2014, when I went to work, my supervisor told me that I had a phone call from downtown and he gave me the information. I called the number and learned that it was the Director of the Examination Unit that had called me. She stated that there was an error in the application of the final answer key and I did not fail the exam but had actually passed it and she gave me my list numbers! I hollered in her ear, "Thank you, Jesus!" then I began to cry! I was so overwhelmed with joy with what the Lord had done!

In April of 2015, I was promoted to a Senior Court Clerk and I give God all of the glory! Everyone said that they had never heard of anything like this ever happening before, but look at God!

One Wednesday night, right before my birthday, I went to church. Our pastor was laying hands on everybody and I remember asking the Lord to please do something special for me. When I went up, my pastor always used to say in my ear, "Tell Him you love Him!" and then I would and the anointing would fall all over me! As I went back to my seat praising God, the Lord spoke to me ever so sweetly and said, "You're going to be among the next generation of Missionaries."

I began to really praise God and to thank Him for even speaking to me in such a profound way! I always knew that I was called to be a Missionary, but for the Lord to speak that into my spirit was amazing! When service was over, one of the Senior Missionaries was coming up the aisle. She grabbed me and began to sing in my ear, "Let the church say Amen, let the church say Amen, God has spoken, so let the church say Amen!" She didn't know that the Lord was using her at that very moment to confirm what He had just given me!

One thing I can surely say about the Holy Ghost is that He will not allow you to continue to live in sin! **"What shall we say then? Shall we continue in sin that grace may abound? God forbid" (Romans 6:1).** The Word of God also lets us know in **Hebrews 12:6, "For whom the Lord loveth he chasteneth, and scourgeth every son whom he receiveth."**

When I look at that last part it makes me think that when you scourge something, you absolutely scrub it clean. Just like the Lord does with us! He scourges every son whom He receives! He scrubs us clean! White as snow, Glory! Don't make me shout up in here!

After a few years of walking in my calling as a Missionary and truly walking in my purpose that the Lord had for me, turning my will over to His Will for my life, I felt in my spirit that the Lord was going to do something for me. I felt that elevation was about to take place, but I was not exactly sure just how it would come. About a week later, I received a call from our Missionary President. She said that the Lord had told her to make me a Missionary Captain. The Lord confirmed it for me and so I accepted the position. I'm sure that there was a lot of inward opposition, but the Lord does all things well!

My very first time being a Captain and rendering a service, the Lord truly blessed us, allowing the anointing to be present and manifested and the souls flocked to the altar! I give my Lord and Savior Jesus Christ all of the glory, honor, and praise! Now, don't get me wrong, it is absolutely not about a title at all! When we get to Heaven, the Lord is not going to call us by "Bishop this" or "Missionary that." Praise God, He is going to call us by our name! The Word of God says in **Romans 3:23, "For all have sinned, and come short of the glory of God."** None of us are perfect and none of us will be perfect until we see Jesus!

Luke 6:41, "And why beholdest thou the mote that is in thy brother's eye, but perceivest not the beam that is in thine own eye?" A lot of times we want to judge our brothers and sisters for the things that they have done because we put a certain stigma on certain sins, but sin is sin and none of it is right in the sight of God!

**"Brethren, if a man be overtaken in a fault,
ye which are spiritual, restore such an one in the
spirit of meekness, considering thyself,
lest thou also be tempted."
(Galatians 6:1)**

I stayed in my mess for longer than I thought I would, but I can truly say that I know Jesus as my DELIVERER!!! I am so grateful for the grace and the mercy of God! Many don't understand my praise because they don't know my story like I know my story (They do now though!). The Lord has since blessed my ex-husband and he found an apartment right across the street from my church and I can say that we are now the best of friends. I know that it's just a matter of time and I am still believing God for him and my children.

**"The Lord shall increase you more and more,
you and your children."
(Psalms 115:14)**

**"For the promise is unto you and to your
children and to all that are afar off, even as
many as the Lord our God shall call."
(Acts 2:39)**

I am now the very proud grandmother of one beautiful granddaughter, and the Lord has since given me so many tremendous testimonies of so many things that He has done in my life! (The next book of my many miracles will be forthcoming!)

If my story offends anybody, or if I have been a stumbling block or hindrance to anyone's walk, I am sorry and I apologize. All I know is that I love Jesus, I am free and I am grateful! I've been redeemed, restored, delivered and set free and I am not the same person that I used to be! We never want to talk about the things that we have done since we have been saved, we just sweep them under the carpet, but I have been delivered from the spirit of shame and I have been released to share my story for God's glory that somebody else could be delivered and set free by the power of the Holy Ghost!

"If the Son therefore shall make you free,
ye shall be free indeed!"
(John 8:36)

I thank and praise God for giving me the courage to be able to share my story with the world. If you are experiencing domestic violence, sexual abuse, physical abuse, drug addiction, bullying, promiscuity, self-gratification, lesbianism, homosexuality, sickness or you or your loved ones are struggling with your salvation or desire to be saved, I want you to know that the blood that Jesus shed for you washes, cleanses, forgives, restores and makes whole!

"Behold, I am the Lord,
the God of all flesh,
is there anything too hard for me?"
(Jeremiah 32:27)

"And blessed is she that believed;
for there shall be a performance of those things which were told her from the Lord."
(Luke 1:45)

"Being confident of this very thing,
that he which hath begun a good work in you will perform it until the day of Jesus Christ."
(Philippians 1:6)

"But as it is written, Eye hath not seen, nor ear heard, neither have entered into
the heart of man, the things which God hath prepared for them that love him."
(1 Corinthians 2:9)

THE MESSED UP MISSIONARY POEM

"And they overcame him
by the blood of the Lamb,
and by the word of their testimony,
and they loved not their lives unto death."
(Revelation 12:11)

There was a time I was bound by sin,
then I opened my heart and let Jesus in!
He washed me clean and changed my name,
a new creature in Him, I wasn't the same!
I walked the walk and lived a holy life,
being a good mother, being a good wife!
I served in the church as a Missionary,
being who God had called me to be!
He snatched me from drugs, lesbianism, and sex,
but unfortunately my husband became my ex!
I was a victim of DV, and also infidelity!
I was so afraid to tell anyone,
Because divorce was something
that just wasn't done!
So I lived my life and told only a few
That I could trust, and wouldn't judge you!
Then sin it got a hold on me,
After I had been set free!
That demon of lust had me bound again,
I found myself sleeping with a female friend.
Don't look at me funny, you have skeletons too,
But it's time to be free, 'cause there's work to do!
He shed His blood and died on the cross,
Just so that we would not be lost!
You don't have to live in shame,
for the Lord has promised to make great your name!

We think in the church that sin doesn't live,
because the secrets we have we refuse to give!
But now it's time to expose the enemy,
that's the only way you'll be set free!
Don't be in church and still be bound,
He wants to turn your life around!
There are some things we refuse to share,
but how much for others do you really care?
This here thing, it's really not about you, deliverance ain't what
you say, it's what you do!
Surrender your will to the Will of God,
Come out of that closet, it's not too hard!
There are people that are waiting to hear your story, so that
Jesus can get all of the glory!
He can do it for you, like He did it for me,
Come on y'all, let's be free!
I know it takes courage to take that stand,
but you will never be bound again!
I was the ***Messed Up Missionary***,
but thank God I can say that now I'm free!

An original, inspired by God and created especially for you by
Tracey L. Ricks © 3/25/17

If You Can't Say It – Let Me Create It!!!

ABOUT THE AUTHOR

Missionary Tracey L. Ricks was born and raised in the Bronx, New York. She is the third of four children raised by her mother, has three children of her own and is the proud grandmother of one beautiful granddaughter.

Her story of abandonment, abuse, drug addiction, abortion and more will have you in tears as you read about the miracle that the Lord has worked in her life. Her's is a story of redemption, hope, deliverance and love, and a testimony to the power of the Holy Ghost through His shed blood on the cross.

She wants everyone who reads her story to know that no matter how far gone you think you are, as long as you still have breath in your lungs, you are not beyond the redemption that the Lord offers.

Tracey stands on the Word of God, and believes that you must be born again, according to **Acts 2:38, "Then Peter said unto them, 'Repent, and be baptized every one of you in the name of Jesus Christ for the remission of sins, and ye shall receive the gift of the Holy Ghost.'"**

Missionary Tracey L. Ricks is a gifted poet and writer, and she gives all the glory for her talents to her Lord and Savior Jesus Christ. One of her favorite passages of Scripture is Psalm 34, and her favorite song is "I Love Jesus."

After reading this book, Tracey hopes that you are encouraged, and remember the words of **Jeremiah 32:27, "Behold, I am the Lord, the God of all flesh: is there anything too hard for me?"**

AUTHOR CONTACT INFORMATION

If you would like to contact Tracey directly:

Phone: 347-674-4830
Email: messedupmissionary01@gmail.com
Website: www.TraceyRicks.com
Facebook - Tracey Ricks